After Hubris, Nemesis:
Why flag carriers fail.

by Simon A. Bennett

Vaughan Paper No. 42

Series Editor: Simon A. Bennett
ISBN: 0 901507 64 4

Institute of Lifelong Learning

© Copyright Institute of Lifelong Learning

All rights reserved. No part of this publication may be reproduced, stored in a retrieval system, transmitted or utilised in any form or by any means, electronic, mechanical, photocopying, recording or otherwise, without permission in writing from the publishers.
Note: Opinions expressed by the author(s) do not necessarily represent those of the Series Editor, the Institute of Lifelong Learning, nor of the University of Leicester, even when an author is a member of its own staff.

First published November 2006

Institute of Lifelong Learning,
University of Leicester,
128 Regent Road,
Leicester LE1 7PA
Tel: 0116 252 5911
Email: lifelonglearning@le.ac.uk
website: www.le.ac.uk/lifelonglearning

British Library cataloguing in publication data
A catalogue record for this book is available from the British Library

ISBN: 0 901507 64 4

Printed in Great Britain by the AnchorPrint Group Limited

For Paul Selby, a gentle-man, much missed.

good bye

Swissair fliegt seit 31. März nicht mehr. Swissair dankt Ihnen - auch im Namen aller Mitarbeiterinnen und Mitarbeiter - für Ihre Treue und Verbundenheit während über 71 Jahren und wünscht Ihnen alles Gute.

Die Meilen, die Sie als Qualiflyer Mitglied mit Swissair gesammelt haben, bleiben gültig (im Rahmen der allgemeinen Geschäftsbedingungen). Mehr unter www.qualiflyer.com.

Swissair cessera de voler le 31 mars. Swissair vous remercie, au nom de ses collaboratrices et collaborateurs, de votre fidélité au cours des 71 années écoulées et vous souhaite tout de bon.

Les miles accumulés en tant que membre Qualiflyer restent valables (selon les conditions réglementaires). Pour de plus amples informations veuillez consulter notre site internet www.qualiflyer.com

Il 31 marzo Swissair esce di scena. Anche a nome di tutti i collaboratori desideriamo ringraziarvi per la fiducia e la simpatia dimostrateci per oltre 71 anni e auguriamo ogni bene.

Le miglia raccolte con il programma Qualiflyer rimangono valide (vedi Condizioni generali di contratto). Maggiori informazioni al sito www.qualiflyer.com

Swissair stopped flying on March 31. Swissair and its employees thank you for your loyalty during the past 71 years. We wish you all the best.

The miles you have collected with Swissair remain valid (according to general terms and conditions). More information at www.qualiflyer.com.

http://www.swissair.com

When I go home
people ask me
Why do you do it? Are you some kind of war junkie?
I won't say a word.
They wouldn't understand why we do it.
They wouldn't understand it's about the man next to you.
That's all it is.
        A soldier's testament, *Black Hawk Down.*[1]

Acknowledgements	1
Management summary	2
1 Introduction — aviation's context	3
1.1 Summary	8
2 Analytical tools	8
3 Assumptions, methodology and structure	12
4 Case study 1: Pan Am	16
4.1 Introduction	16
4.2 Juan Trippe: American hero	16
4.3 Politics and perception	18
4.4 Post-Trippe: instability and adversity	20
4.5 Post-mortem	30
4.6 Observations	30
5 Case study 2: Swissair	33
5.1 Introduction	33
5.2 Swissair — a short history	34
5.3 Swiss: a new beginning	44
5.4 Lufthansa-Swiss: a new beginning revisited	46
6 Case study 3: Sabena	47
6.1 Sabena — a short history	47
6.2 SN: a new beginning	49
6.3 SN-Virgin Express: a new beginning revisited	50
7 Discussion	50
7.1 Pan Am	50
7.2 Swissair/Swiss International Air Lines/Lufthansa-Swiss	55
7.3 Sabena/SN/SN-Virgin Express	58
8 Conclusion	59
8.1 Summary	64
References	65
Appendix	81
The Author	82
Vaughan College publications	82

Acknowledgements

Thanks go to all the pilots who made me feel welcome in their vertical world and who, despite being fatigued, made time to speak with me. Thanks also to Ms Barbara Cassani, Captain Ed Winter, Captain Peter Griffiths and Captain Simon Searle for getting me started in the airline business eight years ago, and Mr Ron Davies for permission to reproduce his Pan Am schematic from *Skygods* by Robert Gandt (1999: 2). The world looks better from 38,000 ft., Mach .78. Majestic. Peaceful. Almost hopeful.

Management summary

Q. Why do flag carriers fail?

A. There are many reasons. They may, for example, develop an inflated sense of self-importance.

Q. Why does this happen?

A. Because:
- state subsidies induce feelings of invulnerability, omnipotence and immortality in management and workers;
- after years as their nation's chosen instrument they lose touch with the realities of the market;
- they come to perceive their own mythologised history as fact (as to how myth can be transformed into fact, read George Orwell's *1984*, specifically his explanation of Newspeak which reflected a single ideology, that of Ingsoc (Orwell, 1949));
- they stop listening ... to the markets, to industry outsiders and insiders, to their employees, to the competition.

Q. How can an airline's management avoid feelings of omnipotence?

A. By:
- listening to customers;
- listening to employees;
- responding to the markets;
- responding to the competition;
- concentrating on core activities ... which for *all* airlines is the provision of safe and economically efficient air transportation;
- guarding against decisions driven by emotion, ego or national fervour;
- being individually reflexive (self-aware).

1 Introduction — aviation's context

> [Aviation is] intensely, vigorously, bitterly, savagely competitive.
> Robert Crandall, cited in Petzinger, 1995: xix.

> [C]ompetition in this market is brutal.
> Willie Walsh, cited in Milner, 2006.

> [E]ach time a new [airliner] programme is launched, management still, in effect, 'bets the company'.
> Christopher Tarry, cited in *Airline Business*, July 2006: 64.

The enterprise of commercial aviation is replete with paradoxes and menace. Glamorous and brutal, chic and unforgiving, in aviation only the strong and clever survive. Aviation is the purest form of commercial Darwinism. As ValuJet discovered when it lost an aircraft over the Everglades, one slip — even by a sub-contractor — can destroy an airline. Aviation's risks are high-consequence.

The terrorist attacks of September 2001 dealt aviation a heavy blow. Some airlines failed. Others went into bankruptcy protection. Even the buoyant low-cost sector suffered. The road to recovery was long and hard. The International Air Transport Association (IATA) estimated that the 2003 Iraq conflict might add as much as $10 billion to airline losses worldwide (*BBC News*, 2003a).

By 2006 the industry seemed to have turned a corner. Then came the Israeli-Hezbollah conflict, a *de facto* civil war in Iraq (Johnson, 2006: 26-29), the re-emergence of the Taliban in Afghanistan, Al Qaeda's global bombing campaign and the August 2006 plot by British-born terrorists to bomb trans-Atlantic carriers (*BBC News*, 2006). The world in 2006 appeared distinctly unstable. Dickey and Nordland (2006: 20-24) claimed the various Middle East conflicts could potentially '... fuel a larger, more amorphous but no less deadly conflict ... '. They described the world as '... far more polarised and interconnected'.

The intersection of instability in the Middle East with rapid economic growth in China and India caused oil prices to soar. In July 2006 Anselmo (2006: 57) observed: 'The spectre of $100 oil couldn't come at a worse time for the U.S. airline industry, which is clawing its way back to profitability after six years of red ink'. In August 2006 *Airliner World* commented: 'With traffic growth starting to cool off and oil prices skyrocketing, the industry could be on the cusp of a downturn' (2006: 9). Reviewing the industry's prospects in the early months of 2006 the head of the International Air Transport Association claimed the industry was going through 'the worst crisis in our history' (Bisignani, cited in Cronin, 2006). Major US carriers staggered in and out of Chapter 11 bankruptcy protection, running up huge debts: 'The US airline industry has largely failed to recover from the downturn following the September 11th terror attacks, while higher fuel prices have added to the desperate situation faced by many airlines. Losses in the US airline sector for 2005 are set to widen to $10 billion from $9.1 billion in the previous year, according to the IATA' (Cronin, 2006).

Despite these pessimistic assessments there were grounds for optimism, however. The industry was more resilient in 2006. Following the post-September 11th slump carriers had reduced their costs (Anselmo, 2006: 57). At the end of 2001 British Airways (BA) was on its knees. In August 2006 BA reported pre-tax profits of £195 million for the three months to the end of June. In November 2005 easyJet reported a 9 per cent rise in profits despite its fuel costs rising by nearly 50 per cent (Cronin, 2006). Osborne (2006: B2) claimed the attempted bombing campaign of August 2006 would have little long-term impact on the sector's valuation: 'Maybe the markets are becoming progressively sanguine about the perennial threat of terrorism. Of course yesterday [August 10th] knocked the share prices of the airlines ... and anyone dependent on the tourist pound. However, investors have already recovered from much worse — 9/11, the Madrid bombings, London's 7/7. On each occasion, the recovery has been quicker'. Market analyst Jim Wood Smith (cited in Quinn and Litterick, 2006: B1) concurred: 'The market has learned how to react to days like this [August 10th] since 9/11 and the shockwaves should be short-lived'.[2] The aircraft manufacturing sector is also more resilient (Barrie, 2006: 36).

As mentioned above, aviation is replete with paradoxes. It contributes both to the taking of life — for example, by unwittingly transporting drugs mules — and to the saving of life by delivering humanitarian aid to disaster zones. Aviation is an environmental 'bad' (it generates noise pollution, devours land, adds to traffic congestion and contributes to global warming) but an economic good. As the world's largest industry it drives scientific and technological innovation and employs vast armies of people, from aircraft designers and craftsmen to pilots and aircraft cleaners. In Switzerland it is estimated that for every airport job, three are generated in the economy (*Neue Zürcher Zeitung*, 2001). Aviation is a *jobs multiplier*.

In Britain commercial aviation has been growing four times faster than the national economy. It sustains 550,000 jobs and contributes over £10 billion each year to the UK's gross domestic product (Virgin Atlantic, cited in *Airliner World*, 2002a). Aircraft manufacturing also contributes significant sums to the Exchequer (although BAe Systems may eventually relocate its manufacturing operation). According to Barrie (2006: 36): 'Employment within the [UK aerospace sector] is now at 124,237, with salaries 31.6% above the manufacturing average'. Over the past twenty years the number of airlines in Europe has risen from 84 to 247 (Phillips, 2005). Globally, the industry is a key economic driver: 'In 1998 the industry provided at least 28 million jobs .... By the year 2010 aviation's economic impact could exceed US$1,800 billion, with over 31 million jobs provided' (ATAG,

2000). In 2000 the Director General of Airports Council International (ACI) observed:

> Air transport and the many industries which support it, contributes more to world GDP than any other industry or service. Besides providing high levels of employment this industry provides both investment opportunities and public service vital to an increasingly global economy (Howe, cited in ATAG, 2000).

The topography of aircraft manufacturing is both a symptom and driver of globalisation. As Sparaco (2006a: 53) explains: 'The aerospace industry is truly global, and, although prime contractors [like BAe Systems and Boeing] retain a clear identity, major programmes are now cross border undertakings transcending geographical, economic and political limits'. Besides being an economic good, commercial aviation is a *social* good, creating opportunities for recreation and cultural exchange. Given the antagonisms of our multi-polar world, aviation's role as an educator should not be underestimated. As a means to personal freedom commercial aviation reproduces the Enlightenment spirit (Bennett, 2001b; 2006).

Because aviation is so important it is vital that we understand why airlines fail. This paper focuses on the collapse of three flag carriers: Pan American World Airways, for many decades the United States of America's *de facto* flag carrier, Swissair and Sabena. The failure of these airlines caused major social, political and economic perturbations. Using Pauchant and Mitroff's (1988) model of the 'crisis-prone' organisation, this paper seeks to explain why these venerable institutions failed. The analysis might help the industry avoid further damaging collapses.

Failure, whether individual, technological or corporate, is a complex phenomenon. It often arises out of unforeseeable interactions between system components or systems. The seeds of failure may be sown years — decades, even — before collapse. Failure may originate in a complex interplay between social, economic and political factors (Vaughan, 1996; Bennett, 2001a). Consequently the more multi-dimensional one's analysis of failure the better one's chances of preventing a repeat.[3] With regard to Pan Am this paper complements the work of Sipika and Smith (1992), Robinson (1994) and Gandt (1999). Sipika and Smith (1992: 3) '... examine[d] the demise of Pan Am within the context of a number of models of turnaround management'. Robinson produced a historical account and Gandt, a retired Pan Am captain, wrote about the airline and his colleagues. Uniquely, the present paper applies Pauchant and Mitroff's (1988) discourse on 'organisational identity' to the demise of Pan Am, Swissair and Sabena.

Pauchant and Mitroff noted a correlation between a corporation's 'concept of self' and its crisis-preparedness and resilience:

> Organisations are often unaware of some of the most important forces influencing their actions .... Interviews [revealed that] only 10 [companies out of 23] had a relatively integrated crisis management plan .... The 'concept of self' or 'organisational identity' appears to be paramount in influencing strategic actions in crisis management. Many organisations need to be encouraged to examine their basic sense of identity (1988: 53).

This paper will ascertain to what degree Pan Am, Swissair and Sabena approximated Mitroff and Pauchant's model of the 'crisis-prone' organisation. Inferences will be drawn where appropriate. As to how the paper might be categorised, it is fundamentally a study of Pan Am, Swissair and Sabena as *social products*. The activity that is commercial aviation is *socially produced*. We have argued elsewhere (Bennett, 2001a: iii) that commercial aviation is the product of the 'vision and labours' of aircraft designers and fabricators, pilots, cabin crew, ground staff, air traffic controllers and many others. Hudson and Pettifer (1979: 6-7) comment: '[T]he history of aviation is not only or chiefly about aeroplanes. It concerns people, too, the people who, in their many different jobs, have made the airlines work ... ' or, sometimes, not work.

1.1 Summary

Commercial aviation, which has both positive and negative impacts, exists in a turbulent environment in which only the most efficient airlines survive. This paper uses Pauchant and Mitroff's theory of the 'crisis-prone organisation' to offer an explanation for the failure of Pan Am, Sabena and Swissair. Although venerable, iconic institutions with a highly developed self-image, none seemed comfortable with deregulation.

Since the attacks of September 11th, 2001, many airlines have improved their productivity. Some, however, still rely on state subsidy (which may be indirect (Cronin, 2006)). Such carriers may be vulnerable to increased competition, rising oil prices or the privatising instincts of their respective governments.

2 Analytical tools

In their work on corporate attitudes to crisis management, Mitroff *et al.* identify 'organisational culture' as a determining factor. The organisational culture, 'tone' or 'mind-set' of an organisation is defined by them as '... the set of rarely articulated, largely unconscious beliefs, values, norms and fundamental assumptions that the organisation makes about itself, the nature of people in general and its environment' (Mitroff *et al.*, 1989: 271). According to Pauchant and Mitroff (1988: 54) organisational culture has a tacit or 'unconscious' quality that may be equated to human personality. As they put it, '... *culture is to an organisation what personality is to an individual* ... some of [an organisation's] most important aspects are unconscious. As a result, organisations are largely *un*aware of some of the most important forces influencing their actions'. In a survey of organisations' crisis management (CM) plans the authors noted a correlation between organisational culture and preparedness:

One fundamental conclusion emerged repeatedly. What differentiates between corporations with weak and strong efforts in CM was the nature of their *'organisational identity'*. By this we mean that how executives feel about themselves and their organisation is strongly related to their firm's involvement in CM.

In their survey Pauchant and Mitroff discovered that '57% of the sample ... had no or only fragmented efforts in CM [and that] *one third had practically no plans whatsoever*'. This finding led them to discriminate two different organisational forms, each with a distinct mind-set. In one, the 'positive self-regard corporation' (PSRC), staff and management care as much for their environment (composed of, amongst other things, customers) as they do for themselves. In the other, the 'self-inflated corporation' (SIC), staff and managers are 'essentially narcissistic', caring 'only or mainly about themselves'. In short, where the PSRC corporation is outward-looking, the SIC corporation is inward-looking and self-centred. In the PSRC corporation customers are valued both as customers and 'fellow human beings'. In the SIC corporation they are viewed only as a means to sustaining the corporation. As Pauchant and Mitroff (1988: 57) explain:

> When asked to list their primary stakeholders, the SIC group has the tendency to emphasise the importance of its *internal* stakeholders such as partners, managers, top management, CEO, etc., while the PSRC group adds to this list *external* stakeholders.

According to Pauchant and Mitroff (1988: 57-58) when confronted with a crisis situation, the SIC group 'uses a great number of *defensive mechanisms*'. These include denial ('the *conscious refusal* to acknowledge reality'), disavowal (where a 'threatening reality' is downplayed), fixation ('a rigid commitment to a particular course of action'), intellectualisation (where a company is so convinced of its social utility and beneficence that it cannot conceive of itself as a target for malcontents), grandiosity (feelings of 'omnipotence, perfection and all-powerfulness') and idealisation ('the feeling of omnipotence through the idealisation of another'). An example of this last defensive mechanism would be the lionisation of a Chief Executive Officer (CEO). According to Mitroff *et al.*'s 'Onion Model of Crisis Management', such 'deep beliefs [and] defensive mechanisms' constitute the 'core organisational identity' of the corporation, and influence 'organisational assumptions/beliefs', 'organisational structure' and 'organisational plans, actions, and behaviour' (Mitroff *et al.*, 1989: 272) . The outermost layers, composed of tangibles like crisis management plans, are easier to observe than the innermost layers. As Mitroff *et al.* put it: '[T]he deepest layers, particularly the core, are the hardest to observe directly' (1989: 273). The 'deepest layers' constitute the organisation's 'core organisational identity' and consist of 'deep beliefs, anxieties [and] defensive mechanisms' (Mitroff *et al.*, 1989: 272). The 'kernel' is composed of the 'character of the individuals working for the organisation' (Pauchant and Mitroff, 1992: 49). With respect to measures of organisational health and survivability, Mitroff *et al.* (1989: 273) take the onion analogy to its logical organic conclusion:

> [T]he factors which constitute the core are often the most decisive .... [I]f the core of an organisation is in trouble — or in common parlance 'rotten' — then the surface activities (behaviour, policies) of an organisation will count for little ... the health of the entire onion [corporation] is often no better than that of its core.

Regarding an organisation's possible 'deep beliefs [and] defensive mechanisms' (the 'core' of the onion) Mitroff *et al.* (1989: 277) identify seventeen 'faulty organisational assumptions/beliefs'. These include, in their own words, 'The fallacy of size: our size will protect us', 'The fallacy of protection/resource abundance: another entity will come to our rescue or absorb our losses', 'The fallacy of excellence: excellent/well managed companies do not have crises', 'The fallacy of location/geography: we don't have to worry about terrorism in the US', 'The fallacy of immunity/limited vulnerability: certain crises only happen to others'. According to Mitroff and Pauchant an organisation's behaviour can be influenced both by 'the context in which [it] competes, the structure of its industry ... its capital and plant requirements' *and* 'much less observable, largely unconscious' organisational assumptions and beliefs (1990: 82). If those assumptions and beliefs are 'faulty' (in a relative, if not an absolute sense) it follows that the organisation may be unable to overcome adversity.

In their book *We're So Big and Powerful Nothing Bad Can Happen to Us* Mitroff and Pauchant (1990: 81-99) explore the 'fallacy of size' and 'the fallacy of protection and resource abundance' through the testimony of corporate executives. As they assert: '... the real proof ... lies "in the words"'. Regarding the first 'fallacy' they comment:

> At its root, the belief that the size of one's organisation will protect it from a major crisis is a crude, but nonetheless, blunt expression of the arrogance of power. Alternate expressions reveal this sentiment even more strongly: 'Our sheer size will shield us from a major crisis'; 'We're so big and powerful that in reality nothing could actually bring us down' (1990: 86).

Regarding the second 'fallacy' the authors comment that organisations that subscribe to the view that someone 'bigger and better' will bail them out '... have grown up and lived most of their existence in a regulated or quasi-regulated environment' (Mitroff and Pauchant, 1990: 88-89). According to Mitroff and Pauchant (1990: 89), 'Utilities and organisations such as ... airlines ... are typically the ones that have not only subscribed to this belief historically but have even prospered as a consequence of holding it'.

3 Assumptions, methodology and structure

A flag carrier is the reification of national will. A flag carrier is national ambition made tangible. A flag carrier is a *political instrument* first and an airline second. Dienel and Lyth (1998: 1-12) assert:

> The people of Belgium, Holland and Switzerland, as much as those of Britain, France and Germany, have developed a strong degree of familiarity, and even affection, for their flag carrier .... [T]he flag carrier's *style* has retained an institutional rather than corporate appearance and they have often been seen by their customers as a part of government .... *Europe's airlines have become embedded in the tapestry of nation states* .... [C]ivil aviation policy in most European countries has included a variety of objectives ... the most common being *the maintenance of air routes for political and strategic reasons* (emphasis added).

According to Dienel and Lyth, while flag carriers have not been entirely un-commercial in their outlook, '... many of their services and managerial decisions have been influenced by the need to maintain national prestige or pursue a political objective [like supporting indigenous industries or serving the needs of the British Empire (framed today as the Commonwealth)]'.

Speaking about the historic role of the flag carrier Calder (2002b) asserts: 'Airlines were mostly run by governments for the benefit of national prestige, foreign policy and staff. High fares prevailed. With the state coffers obliged to meet any deficit, there was little incentive for efficiency. A web of anti-competitive restrictions meant that the private sector struggled to survive'. Britain's Imperial Airways devoted much effort to serving the needs of Empire. The Empire Flying Boats delivered diplomatic mail and diplomats to the Middle East and beyond (Bennett, 2006). BOAC's post-War aircraft like the de Havilland Comet and Bristol

Britannia carried the Union Flag on their tail adjacent to the 'Speedbird' logo (Middleton, 1986). According to Ashworth (1991: 86-88 and 144-148), BOAC and BEA put service before profit.[4] They bought British-manufactured aircraft. A BOAC Chairman once remarked, in Ashworth's words, that '... he never believed it was the Corporation's job to make profits, the Corporation was there to support the British aircraft industry' (d'Erlanger, cited in Ashworth, 1991). According to Ashworth (1991: 187) these imperatives constituted 'externally induced inefficiencies'.

Following its privatisation in 1987 BA planned to drop its Speedbird logo. June Fraser, President of the Society of Industrial Artists and Designers, protested: 'It is alarming that the corporate identity proposed for *our national airline*, relying as it does upon a barely distinguishable heraldic device ... should shortly ... *be the image of this country on the tarmacs of the world* (emphasis added)' (Fraser cited in Lovegrove, 2000: 118). Clearly, despite the Thatcher government's privatising instincts, BA had a special significance for the Establishment.

Ten years later BA was still lauded as 'the UK's flag airline' (Taylor, 1997: 66). In an article dated November 6th, 2001, the *Daily Telegraph* referred to BA as Britain's 'Flag carrier' (Osborne, 2001). In its February 5th, 2002 edition the *Daily Express* called BA 'the national carrier' (Richards, 2002). In February 2002 Calder (2002a) described BA as a 'national institution', one of Britain's 'emblems of nationhood'.

Financial Times journalists Done and Dombey (2001) assert: 'Aviation remains tangled in a web of ... strong emotions. Sovereign countries ... continue to be as attached to the idea of having a national airline as they are to having a flag and a national anthem'. The *Independent* (*Outlook*, 2001) put broadly the same view: 'Nearly every country in the world has one of these national totems [flag carriers] which ... have become like another branch of international diplomacy. They only exist because of the pretensions of governments ... '. National airlines confirm statehood.

Consequently, say Fleck *et al.* (2001: 6-7) they occupy '... a crucial place in a nation's heart. Air France, British Airways, American Airlines, Alitalia — they all hold a special significance to their countries'. According to McRae (2001) this 'special significance' was so pronounced in Belgium and Switzerland that; 'When Swissair and Sabena ran into financial difficulties, it became a symbol of Swiss and Belgian national ills'. McRae states: 'Airlines are hugely symbolic .... They remind us of the still-enormous power of nationalism, for unlike trains or cars, aircraft bear flags and brand themselves with national signs'. Flag carriers serve to broadcast a nation's values and aspirations. As the director of *Grounding*, the 2006 film that documented Swissair's collapse, observed:

> In the end Swissair wasn't about business .... It was about our national identity and Swiss values: organisation, precision, being fair. Switzerland is a small country, and we saw Swissair as our message of these values to the rest of the world (Steiner, cited in Foulkes, 2006).

An enduring feature of the world's flag carriers has been their unprofitability. McMullan states: 'Some [flag carriers] are financial basket cases ...' (cited in Barter, 2001). Doganis asserts: 'It is clearly the case that there are far too many flag carriers in Europe' (cited in Barter, 2001). Reviewing the chronic inability of CSA Czech Airlines, LOT Polish Airlines and Malev Hungarian Airlines to make money, Mosner notes: 'Being state-owned can make it very challenging to adapt to changing market conditions' (cited in Flottau, 2006: 42). Flottau (2006: 42) says: '[C]ost-cutting remains a challenge in legacy structures'. By August 2006 the Hungarian government had made seven attempts to sell its flag carrier, Malev. Close to a deal on one occasion, the state was thwarted by union resistance. Mosner (2006: 44) comments: '[Malev] can no longer afford to be a tool for political benefit and has to be run purely as a business'.

But do flag carriers need to make money? Dienel and Lyth observe: 'Undertakings in which governments have invested a lot of tax-payers' money and which literally carry the flag, are rarely allowed to crash ... '. Campbell and Kingsley-Jones (2002) comment: 'While many flag carrier airlines are now nominally outside state control, there are ... often strong links between airline and state'. British Airways, for example, is still constructed as Britain's flag carrier (see above) despite Virgin Atlantic's conspicuous use of the Union Flag on its long-haul aircraft.

This paper uses the deductive method to evaluate how closely the demise of Pan Am, Swissair and Sabena approximate Pauchant and Mitroff's model of the 'crisis-prone' organisation. The case studies contain some primary data in the form of quotations from Pan Am, Swissair and Sabena employees — although the quotations are garnered from secondary sources (books and news items).

Following a brief introduction the Pan Am case study discusses Juan Trippe's influence on the airline he founded (Section 4.2). Trippe's personality and his impact on contemporaries are discussed. In Section 4.3 Pan Am's self-perception and standing with opinion-formers and the American public are explored. In Section 4.4 Pan Am's performance after Trippe's departure is reviewed. The impact on the company of airline deregulation and of Pan Am's several Chief Executive Officers are discussed. Section 4.5 reviews the airline's demise. The case study concludes with observations on the corporation, its character, expansion, contraction and death.

The second case study opens by locating Swissair's bankruptcy in relation to the terrorist attacks of September 11th, 2001 (Section 5.1). Section 5.2 reviews Swissair's history and, as with the Pan Am case study, draws a picture of the airline as a social, economic and political artefact. It also describes Swissair's chronic financial problems and the impact of the post-September 11th economic turbulence. Section 5.3 describes the reasons for, and nature of, Swissair's resurrection in the form of Swiss International Air Lines. Section 5.4 describes Swiss International Air Lines's Lufthansa-sponsored resurrection. The case study of Sabena follows the same format.

Section 7 seeks to explain the chronic decline of the three airlines, including the impact of Lockerbie and the Gulf War on Pan Am, and the impact of the September 11th attacks on Swissair and Sabena. Section 8 has two objectives: first, to draw lessons from the analysis presented here, and secondly, to encourage the world's airlines to examine their policies and priorities in the light of the disappearance of three of the world's most prominent carriers.

4 Case study 1: Pan Am

4.1 Introduction

Following Mitroff *et al's*. dictum that '... the deepest layers, particularly the core, are the hardest to observe directly' (1989: 273), the following analysis is intended to reveal the 'soul' of Pan Am.

4.2 Juan Trippe: American hero

The airline was founded in 1927 by Juan Trippe. Trippe retired in 1968. According to Davies, Trippe demonstrated '... a masterly grasp of international affairs, both business and political .... His vision of the ultimate possibilities of transport aircraft was ahead of his time'. Trippe 'turned the name Pan American into a household word around the world' (Davies, 1972: 533). Under Trippe's tutelage the airline benefited from '... visionary planning, organisational élan [and] solid infrastructure .... For half a century, Pan Am led and the rest of the airline world followed' (Davies, 1987: 86). According to Branson (2001: 1) Trippe '... almost single-handedly built a world airline ... *but often acted as if he owned the world* (emphasis added)'. Gandt (1999: x) asserts: 'Trippe ... was the ultimate Skygod. Under his direction, Pan Am ruled the airline world with almost divine authority'. Bender and Altschul comment: 'Trippe was a zealot whose religious faith was commercial air routes, a visionary who saw the future ... *and claimed it for Pan American Airways in perpetuity* (emphasis added)' (1982: 15).

Juan Trippe's vision was simple. He intended '... to provide mass air transportation for the average man [sic] at rates he can afford to pay' (Trippe, cited in University of Miami, 1996). Trippe's company made record profits. According to Sampson (1984: 124) Pan Am became the 'dominating influence' in American aviation (although Trans World Airlines (TWA) was a determined rival (Bremner, 1990: 20)). The airline expanded its route network and introduced modern aircraft like the Boeing 307 Stratoliner (the first pressurised passenger aircraft) and Boeing 314A flying boat (Hudson and Pettifer, 1979: 113-114). Trippe was ambitious. 'Pan American ... want all the business' remarked Roosevelt (Roosevelt cited in Bender and Altschul, 1982: 12). Commercial aviation expanded rapidly. In 1945 civil airlines carried nine million passengers. By 1993 (two years after Pan Am's bankruptcy) they carried 1.17 billion (Brookes, 1996: 7).

For the majority of the post-War period Washington's Civil Aeronautics Board (CAB) sought to control the direction and scale of development of US civil aviation. Seat prices and routes were regulated (Petzinger, 1995: 15-19). The CAB told Pan Am it had 'too many employees per passenger' (CAB cited in Flanagan, 2000). While airlines were free to initiate technological developments, the CAB adjudicated their relationship with the customer.[5] According to Sampson (1984: 133-135) within a system driven by patronage the CAB 'tried to protect airlines from heavy losses or bankruptcy'. Trippe disliked regulation. As Branson explains:

> Before anyone else [Trippe] believed in airline travel as something to be enjoyed by ordinary mortals .... In 1945 other airlines didn't think or act that way. Trippe decided to introduce a 'tourist class' fare from New York to London. He cut the round-trip fare [by]

more than half .... This went over like a lead balloon in the industry ... it didn't want to hear about the tourist class (2001: 1).

Innovations abounded: '[Pan Am] introduced around-the-world service in 1947, direct flights to South America in 1948, low-cost tourist fares in 1952, trans-Atlantic jets in 1958, around-the-world jets in 1959, and jet air freighters in 1963' (National Aviation Hall of Fame, 1997). Having persuaded Boeing to build the models, Pan Am was the first carrier to fly both the Boeing 747 and the long-range 747SP ('special performance'). For a decade Pan Am operated more 747s than anyone else (Lucas, 1981: 77-79). The 747 gave commercial aviation a tremendous boost: 'The 747 established new operating and business rules ... and ... significantly contributed to the ascendancy of commercial aviation' (Sparaco, 2006b: 53). Pan Am introduced the first global processor-based reservation system (PANAMAC) and pioneered computer-based engine monitoring. It made the first fully automated approach and landing with a scheduled service. It was the first to downlink engine performance data to a ground station (Pan American World Airways History, 2000). By the mid-1960s Pan Am was the world's largest international airline. The 1966 annual report showed that profits had risen over 60 per cent from the previous year. Trippe considered retiring from his 'tribute to private enterprise' (Bender and Altschul, 1982: 508).

4.3 Politics and Perception
Pan Am aligned itself closely with Washington. According to Sampson (1984: 78-84) 'Trippe ... depicted himself as a great American patriot, enabling his nation through its *chosen instrument* to spread its influence round the world .... [He] liked to explain that his airline was helping to save the world for democracy ... (emphasis added)'.[6] According to one source 'Every American President ... consulted the company, and world leaders often confided in Pan Am *as if it were the US government* (emphasis added)' (Io Communications, 2001). Trippe's patriotism found

overt expression in adverts like the 1941 poster *The Most Watched-For Ship In The World*:

> [T]he Flying Clipper Ships of Pan American ... carry the hopes of democracy everywhere .... [T]he Clippers ... are Uncle Sam's ambassadors of good will. They carry America's traditions of freedom to 55 lands.

Another poster described Pan Am's Boeing Clippers as '... vital as Uncle Sam's strong right arm in furthering US trade and good will' (Duke University, 1999). Pan Am made a major contribution to the war effort: 'Pan Am carried military personnel and cargo; ferried bombers and aircraft; and built fifty airports in fifteen countries. The airline also trained thousands of military pilots, navigators and mechanics' (University of Miami, 1996). Trippe's desire to 'save the world for democracy' resonated with politicians (Ambrose, 1985; Maidment and McGrew, 1991). The public-private partnership continued throughout the Cold War: 'In the early 50s, Pan Am was awarded contracts for the operation of the Eastern Test Range, a NASA missile tracking operation ... and the new NASA base at (then) Cape Canaveral, Fla.' (Flanagan, 2000). The US government chose Pan Am to run its Internal German Service (IGS).

At the end of the 1960s Pan Am reached its apogee. As Petzinger (1995: 17) puts it: 'Second only to Coca-Cola in worldwide recognition, the Pan Am trademark had become a fixture of popular culture, symbolising the exotic .... A spaceship bore the Pan Am trademark in *2001: A Space Odyssey* [American Stanley Kubrick's space adventure film] .... Pan Am built the largest commercial office building in the world [located in New York, helicopters operated from its roof] ... '. Wilkinson (1991) ventures that Pan Am was 'A national treasure, Pan Am became part of popular culture. In the fifties, Norman Rockwell illustrated Pan Am ads. Ernest Hemingway told *Look* magazine readers: "Pan Am and I are old friends"' (Wilkinson cited in Deppa, 1993: 224). In Lovegrove's (2000: 114) opinion

Pan Am's blue globe logo hinted at global domination. According to Sipika and Smith (1992: 9) Pan Am '... operated in much the same way as "national" airlines like British Airways and Air France'. Robinson (1994: ix) asserts: '[Pan Am was] America's "Chosen Instrument" in international aviation'. It was a 'faux' flag carrier in competition with official flag carriers like the British Overseas Airways Corporation (BOAC) (Dienel and Lyth, 1998: 1). According to Davies (1987: 82) Pan Am enjoyed a '... *de facto* monopoly of international US air traffic'. Rendall (1988: 149) asserts: 'Pan American was just what the US government needed: a highly efficient business, innovative in its use of aircraft and the latest aviation technology, with a vigorous man at the top. It became a 'chosen instrument' ... almost an extension of US foreign policy ... '. Trippe was rewarded for his contribution to aviation and America's global standing. In President Truman's opinion Pan Am's technological innovation had 'won the war' for America (Truman cited in Robinson, 1994: ix). He gave Trippe the Medal of Merit. Pan Am's creator became America's most decorated citizen.

4.4 Post-Trippe: instability and adversity [7]

Until Edward Acker's appointment in 1981 Pan Am suffered 'four hapless chief executives', claims Petzinger (1995: 186). The oil shock of 1973 and accompanying recession hit the airlines hard (Bennett, 2006).[8] Pan Am's long-haul flights lost large sums: 'For the airlines it was the ultimate absurdity, at a time of exorbitant fuel costs and financial crises, to be flying huge empty planes round the world ... ' (Sampson, 1984: 127).

It is debatable whether Pan Am could have foreseen such problems, however. The Boeing 707 had been a commercial success.[9] Enthused, Trippe urged Boeing's Bill Allen to build an aircraft two-and-a-half times the size. His order for the 747 was valued at $US550 million. The aircraft was a technological marvel ... but an economic nightmare. According to Branson (2001: 3) '... the 747 ... sank Pan Am'. Strict seat price controls in conjunction with the recession of the early 1970s meant that airlines like

Pan Am were unable to attract a more economically diverse public. According to Petzinger (1995: 18) 'The Boeing 747 ... McDonnell Douglas DC-10 and Lockheed L-1011 ... would devastate the airline industry .... The planes were simply too big'. Pan Am attempted to borrow from the Shah of Iran.

Two years after Trippe's retirement the airline business had its worst year ever. The airlines tried to turn themselves around by discounting certain fares and offering different levels of service. The regulatory context, however, remained almost unchanged (Doganis, 1991: 48). The CAB directed business. Most travellers stuck to the train, coach or car (Petzinger, 1995: 18-20). (The International Air Transport Association was as interventionist as the CAB. IATA was '... effectively a suppliers' cartel, whose object was to maximise its members' profits by mutually fixing the prices at which they sold their services' (Doganis, 1991: 38)).

Consumerism, however, changed everything. Championed by the Carter Administration and entrepreneurs like Britain's Frederick ('Freddie') Laker, consumerism hit TWA, National and Pan Am hard. In 1977 Freddie Laker launched his 'Skytrain' no-frills service across the North Atlantic.[10] For a while Skytrain was a success (Hudson and Pettifer, 1979: 196-197). According to Petzinger (1995: 187-188) Pan Am was unconcerned: 'Pan Am ... *arrogantly turned up its nose* at Laker, uninterested in trying to capture the backpacking bargain customer (emphasis added)'.[11] In Petzinger's view the major problem was Pan Am's culture. 'Pan Am', asserts Petzinger, '[was] a company practically frozen by *the inertia of grandeur and tradition* (emphasis added)'.

The 1978 Airline Deregulation Act (ADA) saw the elimination of the CAB and of 'all controls over routes and fares [within the US]'. Carter was determined that the benefits of deregulation should also be brought to international air travel:

Carter ... had a fundamental belief in the benefits of greater competition. The early stages of domestic deregulation in the United States appeared to be producing lower fares for consumers and higher airline profits without any marked instability for the industry. *The protected position of Pan American ... could not be justified.* If greater competition was proving beneficial domestically, it would also do so internationally (emphasis added) (Doganis, 1991: 53).

According to Sipika and Smith (1992: 9) whereas Pan Am had been '... largely insulated from the ravages of the free market' the Act '... left Pan Am severely exposed and open to increased competition'. Hudson and Pettifer (1979: 199) claim the ADA inverted the industry: '[T]he image that airlines ... were selling was no longer elegance and service or even punctuality; it was value for money .... Mass travel had arrived in a way which surprised even the Americans'. Ball (1986) comments: 'Travellers [were] offered airline speed at Greyhound Bus fares. A marked slippage in services [was] the price'.

Previously the CAB had kept seat prices high (believing this would compensate for poor load factors). With the CAB's controls removed the airlines found themselves in a price war — both within and without the USA.[12] Pan Am fought back, introducing a more flexible pricing structure (Hudson and Pettifer, 1979: 206). In order to gain more control over feeder services it agglomerated, buying National Airlines in 1979.[13] 'Pan Am management [did] a poor job of integrating National into Pan Am's operations' claims Robinson (1994: 172-173). 'Miscellaneous expenses' increased by 74 per cent. In 1978/79 oil prices broke all records (Sentance, 2001). By the end of the decade trading conditions were very difficult. Interest rates approached 20 per cent. Inflation was well over 10 per cent. New entrants like People Express fuelled the price war (Robinson, 1994: 172).

Pan Am was hamstrung by its culture. It was 'the most heavily unionised [airline] in America' (Petzinger, 1995: 190). According to Petzinger (1995: 190) 'Featherbedding [work-shyness] was legion'. Sipika and Smith (1992: 11) describe the workforce as 'inflexible'. People Express, in contrast, had no unions. Express practised inclusive management. The airline's CEO wanted '... to make everyone feel responsible' (Sampson, 1984: 216). Pan Am was different. Trippe had bequeathed 'an imperial dictatorship, operated with a token nod to twentieth-century principles of management'. One of his successors sacked three dozen senior managers, replacing them with mostly non-airline people (Bender and Altschul, 1982: 518).[14] The sum product was, according to Robinson (1994: 172) 'a bloated and slow-moving "Chosen Instrument"'.

The behaviour of Pan Am's employees bordered on the schizophrenic. When Seawell reduced the workforce from 42,000 to 27,000, Pan Am's flight crew formed AWARE — 'airmen worried about remaining employed'.[15] Gandt (1999: 158) states that AWARE 'quickly swelled beyond the pilot roster'. Employees could also be highly supportive of the company: 'All through this very tough time ... Pan Am employees time and time again accepted wage concessions and did everything they could to help keep the venerable airline aloft' (Robinson, 1994: 174).[16]

Pan Am's workforce was Janus-faced. It cared for Pan Am *the institution* (because it was patriotic and sentimental) but clung to practices that placed the enterprise in jeopardy. Management accepted the need to modernise, but failed to understand that a putsch against its longest-serving managers would damage the airline's 'organisational memory'.

Prior to Acker's arrival, management had sold the lease on the Pan Am building. In 1981 Pan Am sold its InterContinental hotel chain to Grand Metropolitan (Grand-Met) for $500 million.[17] No-one else was invited to bid. Many believed the sale price to be too low. A couple of years later Grand-Met sold the chain for $2 billion. Robinson (1994: 173) attributes this missed opportunity to Pan Am's 'inwardly focused' management. Although imperfectly executed, these divestments helped the airline cut its potential loss for the year from $386.9 million to $18.9 million. Pan Am's loss for 1982 was $485.3 million (Sipika and Smith, 1992: 12). At this time the airline was losing around $1 million each day.

Acker battled on. New services were started and new aircraft purchased.[18] The fleet was rationalised around the various Boeing types. The cargo operation was terminated. Pan Am cut its fares to London by almost 60 per cent. The price war took its toll: '[P]rofits [were] ... devastated across the industry. In the first quarter of 1983 the US airline industry racked up the deepest quarterly deficit in its history, $640 million' (Petzinger, 1995: 185-191). In 1983 Pan Am lost $51 million. In August 1983 the House Subcommittee on Investigations and Oversight said of deregulation: 'Our carriers' viability has been adversely affected by an open skies policy which has extended domestic deregulation to the international arena' (House Subcommittee, cited in Sampson, 1984: 146). Acker commented: 'For Pan Am, the effect [of deregulation] was negative' (cited in Sampson, 1984: 146). (Load factors recovered during the second half of the decade, however (Doganis, 1991: 5)).

Acker restructured. There were route revisions and manpower reductions. Sipika and Smith claim, however, that Acker's initiative was compromised by currency fluctuations, a reduction in passenger-carrying capacity and the price war. Acker bought Airbus Industrie wide-bodied A300 and A310 aircraft, a 'strange move' according to Sipika and Smith (1992: 13).[19] (The airline sold all its US-made widebodies within five years of their acquisition).[20] In 1984 Pan Am lost $US 207 million. Half way through the year Acker conceded '... the job was much worse than I had expected .... I couldn't foresee how the high dollar would add to our problems ... so much of our revenue is in other currencies' (cited in Sampson, 1984: 215). Writing in the same year Sampson (1984: 215) concluded: 'Pan Am still lives in the long shadow of Juan Trippe and *the accretions of imperial splendour* ... (emphasis added)'.

In 1985 Pan Am's unions struck.[21] The airline's finances were in a parlous state. According to Petzinger, Pan Am had been using its pension programmes as a 'piggy bank' and had frozen retirement benefits. (When entrepreneur Robert Maxwell used his company's pension fund 'for his own purposes' there was an outcry (Cook and Stevenson, 1996: 229)). Acker sold Pan Am's Pacific routes — 'a crucial mistake' claim Sipika and Smith (1992: 14). Davies (1987: 84) comments: 'While the Pacific routes were profitable [and] the fastest growing ... it did not make so much money as the Atlantic routes, and Acker had to follow the hard facts ... '. The received wisdom held true. By the early 1990s '... The North Atlantic was the world's largest market' (Dienel and Lyth, 1998: 248). But the Atlantic market is volatile — as British Airways (BA) discovered after the terrorist attacks of September 11th, 2001 (Flight International, 2002b).

When disposing of its Pacific Division Pan Am negotiated with only one party — UAL (parent company of United Airlines). As with InterContinental Pan Am eschewed competitive bidding. UAL paid $750 million for the Pacific Division (23 per cent of Pan Am's network). In 1994 UAL's Pacific operation was valued at around $3 billion. Pan Am's 'inwardly focused' (Robinson, 1994: 173) management had again failed to secure maximum benefit. Pan Am's Pacific Division had been Trippe's 'crowning glory and achievement' claims Robinson. The loss of Pan Am's defining achievement hit time-served employees hard. According to Robinson 'Upon hearing of the sale, many long-time Pan Am employees just cried'. According to Gandt (1999: 216) one pilots' union representative asserted: 'We're cutting off our right arm'. The unions '... were fed up with Acker for the ... sale' (Robinson, 1994: 176-178).

Pan Am's 1985 profit of $452 million became a loss of $469 million in 1986,[22] and a loss of $265 million in 1987. Pan Am's load factors were hit by terrorism,[23] Chernobyl and the US bombing of Libya. The airline owed $1 billion. Cost-cutting generated union unrest. Acker tried to sell Pan Am. This alienated the workforce. At the beginning of 1988 Acker was dismissed. In Gandt's (1999: 221-237) opinion Acker's time at Pan Am was noteworthy for industrial relations so acrimonious that the unions began to demand his dismissal in return for their co-operation. Gandt (1999: 237) offers this summary of Acker's (and his predecessor's) stewardship: 'Ah, the arrogance! The Skygodly loftiness .... Both Seawell and Acker had reigned over the Imperial Airline *like potentates of a medium-sized monarchy* ... (emphasis added)'.

Prior to his departure Acker — 'an itinerant airline manager' according to Gandt — had feuded with Chief Operating Officer Marty Shugrue. Shugrue had started out as a pilot and, at the time of his confrontation with Acker, had been with Pan Am for 20 years. Like the unions Shugrue wanted Pan Am to remain independent. The feud did not help Pan Am's fortunes: 'The board of directors observed the feud with growing horror. It was like watching their own generals slug it out while the enemy was torching the camp' (Gandt, 1999: 235). Industrial relations reached a nadir when Pan Am employees stood outside the Pan Am building chanting 'Jump, Eddie, jump'. Eventually the board fired both men.[24]

Many Pan Am fliers had spent most — if not all — of their career with the airline: '[T]hey had lived their entire adult lives beneath an institutional umbrella — home, college, the military, then the airlines. Not one minute of their lives had been spent languishing in unemployment' (Gandt, 1999: 223). During the mid-1970s Pan Am had released pilots. By the mid 1980s Pan Am was in a position to re-hire pilots. According to Gandt (1999: 225) even the experience of being fired by Pan Am had not impacted pilots' loyalty: 'They wore reading glasses .... Some had established successful new careers [but] [t]hey were coming back to Pan Am because during all those years they thought they were missing something'. Gandt

(1999: 227) describes the mind-set of one pilot (Errol Johnstad, chairman of the pilots' union) thus:

> [He had] become an Eagle Scout, been class president ... then gone on to win his Air Force wings. *He had even become a pilot for Pan American World Airways ... a Maximum Skygod* (emphasis added).

For Johnstad, the employees were the soul of the corporation. '*We* are Pan Am' he said on one occasion (cited in Gandt, 1999: 227).

Edward Acker was succeeded by Thomas Plaskett. A long-serving Pan Am manager, Jeffrey Kriendler, described Plaskett thus: 'Excellent. Very cool. Well spoken. Credible. Smart'. In Gandt's opinion Plaskett was 'Mister Nice Guy'. According to Kriendler (cited in Deppa, 1993: 228-234) Plaskett was shocked by what he found. 'I found a company that was not just weak and foundering. I found a company in utter chaos' said Plaskett (Plaskett cited in Petzinger, 1995: 356). Morris (1988) says that Plaskett '[S]pelled out the hard choices faced by the airline. After a decade of high costs, union strife, big losses and increased competition ... Pan Am had to pull itself out of the doldrums'.

Pan Am was selling seats at a loss (travel agents were taking large commissions). Its aircraft were dirty and outdated and carried the legal minimum number of cabin crew. Deppa (1993: 224) states: 'For five consecutive years, a *Fortune* magazine survey had shown Pan Am among the ten least admired corporations in America'. Writing in 1986 Ball observed: 'Pan American ... used to put 14 flight attendants on a Boeing 747 .... Now there are often 12 and sometimes ten .... [One flight attendant] said that during the Christmas period, some jumbo jets had only eight .... "I can't do three people's work", she said' (1986: 5). Plaskett became 'emotionally vested in the turnaround at Pan Am', says Petzinger (1995: 358). Plaskett re-defined the product. He improved scheduling, comfort and safety. At this time economic conditions were favourable (Doganis, 1991: 342-343).

Following the December 1988 bombing of Flight 103 over Lockerbie concerns were raised about:

a) the age of Pan Am's aircraft (it had the oldest 747 fleet of any airline);

b) its security systems (a 1986 security audit had criticised Pan Am); and

c) its relationship with US government agencies (who had warned civil servants not to fly with Pan Am) (Sipika and Smith, 1992: 17-19).

The bombing exacted a huge toll. As Petzinger (1995: 359-360) explains: 'In a matter of hours the airline lost half its transatlantic bookings .... Practically overnight Plaskett's enthusiasm, his I'm-a-believer rhetoric, had been drained away'. 'The bombing meant dishonour for the airline' claims Deppa (1993: 224). Kriendler claims that 'Lockerbie ... sped the breakup of the company, and thus ultimately its demise' (cited in Deppa, 1993: 236). Regester and Larkin (1997: 146) question Plaskett's response: '[D]id Pan Am's CEO ... go to Lockerbie, apologise, attend memorial services, atone for responsibility? He did not. The media made mincemeat of the airline .... Passengers lost confidence ... and chose other airlines in preference'. Today's received wisdom is that the CEO *must* offer her/his condolences and support to the friends and relatives of the deceased and, if possible, attend the disaster scene. When Comair Flight 5191 (a CRJ-operated internal service) crashed shortly after take-off at Lexington, Kentucky in August 2006, the airline's President immediately held a press conference at which he offered his sympathies and pledged co-operation.

In May of that year Plaskett sold Pan Am World Services, raising $130 million. (Given that World Services was grossing some $500 million annually, the sale would appear short-sighted (Flanagan, 2000)). The

'Lockerbie effect' lasted the whole of 1989, and cost Pan Am $450 million (Sipika and Smith, 1992: 19). Petzinger (1995: 360) comments: 'Suddenly anyone contemplating an international flight on Pan Am — Pan Am, that symbol of American influence across the globe — found himself weighing the odds of survival en route'. Sixteen months after Lockerbie a US commission accused both the FAA and Pan Am of negligence (Sochor, 1991: 152). Smith (1992: 68) observes: 'The process of organisational recovery after a crisis event is not an easy task, as witnessed by ... Pan Am'. 'An airline's revenue is acutely sensitive to recession or security worries' says Avery (cited in Fleck *et al.*, 2001: 6-7).

In commerce, reputation is one of the pillars of success (Hussey and Ong, 1999: 43-47). Plaskett knew he had to restore confidence in his airline. He fought back on two fronts. He refurbished Pan Am's fleet and sought a buyer for the airline. As to the mood of the crews at this time, Gandt (1999: 260-265) notes:

> Among most [pilots] there was a deep-seated conviction that Pan Am wouldn't ... go Tango Uniform ['Tits Up', that is, bankrupt]. Hell, for one thing, they *knew* the government wouldn't allow such a thing .... And all that baloney about astronomic losses ... well, they'd been hearing that twaddle for twenty-five years .... Pan Am pilots could still comport themselves like Skygods.

The 1990/1991 Gulf War secured Pan Am's fate. Fuel costs rose and demand fell (Doganis, 1991: 344). Plaskett sold IGS and resolved to sell the airline's trans-Atlantic routes. After declaring Chapter 11 bankruptcy, the airline was given permission to sell its Heathrow slots. It found itself confined to Miami and South America. By the end of 1991 the rump Pan Am was doomed. 'Who would have thought such a thing could happen?' writes Robinson (1994: xi).[25]

4.5 Post-mortem

Plaskett attributed the airline's death to ' ... its board of directors, its management, its unions, our government, and fate' (cited in Petzinger, 1995: 394). Branson (2001: 3) says Trippe '... failed to reinvent his company for the leaner, far more competitive age he had done so much to shape ...'. In other words, claims Branson, Trippe failed to adjust to the world he helped create. Robinson (1994: ix) comments: 'Pan Am ... tumbled into a morass of mismanagement, financial excess, harmful U.S. government policies, and just sheer bad luck ... '. Pan Am's board of directors failed to give the company the steer it needed. Only when Acker had accumulated $1.7 billion-worth of losses did Pan Am's board act. Pan Am's board was 'sleepy' says Robinson. Another problem was Pan Am's failure to achieve economies of scale, leaving merger 'the only way to survive' (Robinson, 1994: 175).

4.6 Observations

Pan Am never recovered from the loss of its charismatic and able founder, Juan Trippe. Under Trippe's visionary leadership Pan Am innovated: it opened up the Pacific with its Boeing seaplanes, bought the Stratoliner, commissioned the 747, joined BOAC and Air France in their support for Concorde and pioneered tourist fares. Under Trippe Pan Am was courted by the great and the good, from US Presidents to the CEOs of airplane manufacturing companies. Trippe, urbane and patrician, was comfortable in such company. As US aviation's 'old chosen instrument' (Dienel and Lyth, 1998: 247) Pan Am secured important commissions, like the IGS. Pan Am the airline was every bit as glamorous, dynamic and patriotic as its founder Juan Trippe. Pan Am reified his will and character.

According to Branson (2001: 1) Trippe acted 'as if he owned the world'. Pan Am followed Trippe's example. Protected from the uncertainties of free market competition by the CAB Pan Am could indulge its employees and customers. A dynastic style of management was evolved that did not end with Trippe's departure. Like the airline's founder, Gray, Halaby and Seawell were patrician entrepreneurs. 'Aloof and lordly' is how Gandt (1999: 192) describes them. To those further down the hierarchy Pan Am provided comradeship, job satisfaction, career development and handsome reward — in sum an 'institutional umbrella' (Gandt, 1999: 223).

Pan Am's watershed was de-regulation and the abolition of the CAB. Pan Am's last two CEOs, Ed Acker and Tom Plaskett, attempted to change the corporate mind-set from one of dependency and self-indulgence to that of self-sufficiency and economy. Acker broke the patrician mould. According to Donald Burr, founder of no-frills airline People Express, Acker was a 'fighter' who 'believed in confrontation' and in 'telling people what to do' under threat of the sack (cited in Sampson, 1984: 216). Acker was prone to 'icy-blue-eyed tantrums' says Gandt (1999: 237). Inevitably, perhaps, the Acker reign was characterised by 'internecine warring' (Gandt, 1999: 236). Ed Acker, the *arriviste*, found himself confronting 'lifers' like Shugrue. The two men had very different backgrounds. Shugrue had worked his way up the corporate ladder, making and keeping friends. The ex-pilot never forgot his roots and remained 'very popular' with Pan Am's unions. In contrast Acker took long lunches, socialised and bred racehorses (Robinson, 1994: 174). After a honeymoon period (during which AWARE members wore badges that read 'I'm an Acker Backer') Acker fell foul of the unions (although the unrest was not entirely Acker's fault: the unions were annoyed that the government refused to bail them out). Unlike Acker and Plaskett, Pan Am's union members were slow to accept Reaganomics. Bad habits persisted. As Petzinger (1995: 190) notes 'featherbedding was legion'. The 1985 strike was myopic (although employees were provoked).

While the unions did not exactly help the reformers' cause, management did not always act in Pan Am's best interests. The fact that management eschewed competitive tendering when selling InterContinental and the Pacific Division damaged Pan Am. The assets were undervalued, causing

Pan Am to secure the slimmest of yields. The decision to acquire National, an airline whose structure did not complement that of Pan Am, was short-sighted. Having acquired National the failure to integrate the airline into Pan Am's operations was logistically and financially dysfunctional. The acquisition was a drain.

Not all of Pan Am's problems were home-grown, however. By the time the 747 became available passenger numbers were in decline. Aircraft were flying around with empty seats. They were burning expensive kerosene. During the 1980s international terrorism and events like Chernobyl discouraged Americans from visiting Europe (US tourism is vital to many European economies). Reaganomics heralded a decade of dog-eat-dog capitalism. Subsidies, hidden or otherwise, disappeared. The Gulf War impacted passenger numbers on the lucrative North Atlantic run — Pan Am's final refuge.

Of course, Pan Am's troubles were not unique. The entire industry was in a trough. Laker, Braniff and People Express went bankrupt. Airlines like Frontier, Republic and Western were acquired by other airlines, who were themselves taken over. Nineteen ninety-one saw the bankruptcy of both Pan Am *and* Eastern Airlines. Eastern, founded by World War One fighter ace Eddie Rickenbacker, was almost as much of an American institution as Pan Am. (One could argue that Rickenbacker was even more charismatic than Trippe). Pan Am's travails were symptomatic of a general malaise.

Swissair's demise is viewed through the same frame of analysis as that applied to Pan Am. The airline's self-image and standing amongst its citizens is explored. Swissair's re-invention as Swiss International Air Lines and take-over by Lufthansa are also described. By way of 'scene-setting' the terrorist attacks of September 11th are reviewed. As with Pan Am a violent act delivered Swissair's coup de grâce.

5 Case study 2: Swissair

5.1 Introduction

On September 11th, 2001 four commercial aircraft were hi-jacked in the US. Two were flown into the World Trade Centre towers in New York. One was flown into the Pentagon in Washington DC. One crashed in Pennsylvania. Hijackers had forced their way onto the flight decks of the aircraft. The attacks were exhaustively reported. Some news channels carried live coverage. *Flight International* (2001b) commented: '[T]he events on the screen — for many unfolding in real time — were ... so awful that most of us, a week later, are still struggling to take them in. There are images — office workers tumbling from top floors of the twin towers, family snapshots of children aboard the doomed flights, the grotesque remains of one of the world's most famous landmarks — that will haunt us for years'. *The Economist* (2001a) noted that more died on September 11th than in the Japanese attack on Pearl Harbour: 'The appalling atrocities of September 11 — acts that must be seen as a declaration of war not just on America but on all civilised people — were crueller in conception and even more shocking than what happened in Hawaii ... '.

There were secondary effects. Many people stopped flying or delayed trips. Major economic perturbations were experienced in the airline, tourism and aircraft manufacturing industries.[26] The loss of human life, capital and business impacted the insurance industry (Watts, 2001). Some airlines failed, including Midway in the US, Canada 3000 and Australia's Ansett.[27] Sabena[28] and Swissair, venerable European flag carriers, were declared bankrupt. In Britain Gill Airways and British World collapsed.[29] British Airways, saddled with a net debt of £6.56 billion (about three times the value of its assets) lost £65 million to December 2001. In February 2002 BA published *Future Size and Shape* — a recovery strategy (Osborne, 2002).

As with the relationship between Pan Am's history and its resilience, it is assumed that Swissair's history had a bearing on its capacity to accommodate the difficult post-September 11th conditions. If Pan Am was a 'flag carrier' in all but name, Swissair was very much 'Switzerland's airline'. It reified Switzerland's values and projected them across the globe (Schwarz, 2002). As with Pan Am, the objective is to understand how Swissair's flag carrier role and self-image hindered its survival. Swissair's post-September 11th successor Swiss International Air Lines is described to show the persistence of the flag carrier model: the managers at Swiss International Air Lines saw themselves as the custodians of a new flag carrier. A March 26th, 2002 Swiss press release referred to the carrier as '... the new national airline' (Swiss, 2002b). The reinvention of Swissair as Swiss raises the question of what lessons were learned from Swissair's collapse. The fact that Swiss was taken over by Lufthansa suggests that few (or none?) were learned.

5.2 Swissair — a short history

Swissair was set up in 1931. Schwarz (2002) observes: 'There was no question of the airline being self-supporting back then. Initially revenues from flight operations covered only 25 percent of costs .... The remainder was covered by subsidies, both open and concealed'. In 1947 it was designated Switzerland's 'national airline' (although Swissair's aircraft had been flying with the Swiss flag painted on their tailfins since before World War Two). Thirty per cent of the company's shares were held by Swiss public institutions. The airline grew quickly 'taking in such far-flung destinations as Anchorage, Buenos Aires, Brazzaville and Taipei'. Swissair positioned itself as a carrier offering a high-quality product to premium fare passengers (i.e. businesspeople). Swissair anticipated that the resulting premium income would compensate for its high costs and low productivity (Doganis, 1999: 201). In 1988 it paid its Captains and First Officers US$165,300 per annum. Pan Am paid its crews US$85,600 and BA US$84,600. In the same year the best *overall* measure of airline productivity — available tonne-kilometres (ATK) per $1,000 of labour cost — put Swissair at more or less the bottom of the league table of major carriers. In 1988 Swissair's ATK per $1,000 was 3,600. Pan Am's was 10,800 and BA's was 7,000. At the top end of the scale Thai International's ATK per $1,000 was 24,000 (Doganis, 1999: 133-136).

Swissair's 'premium fare, high yield' strategy did not work particularly well. In 1988 the airline made an operating profit of US$11 million only. SAS, an airline with a similar marketing strategy, made a profit of US$223 million. American Airlines made a profit of US$801 million (Doganis, 1999: 201). Swissair survived, however. By 1995 Swissair employed 17,000 people and enjoyed 'an enviable reputation for in-flight service and punctuality' (Trevelyan, 2001). According to Schwarz 'Swissair became a patriotic legend, an ambassador for such Swiss values as reliability, quality, solidity [and] security'. In 1996 Swissair was voted 'Airline of the Year'. But such awards gave a false impression. Swissair moved into the red in the early 1990s and did not move into the black again until 1997. The airline made significant staffing cuts. In 1996 it employed 16,130. In 1997, following a restructuring, it employed 7,335. Pay was frozen. These reforms seemed to work: in 1995 Swissair's load factor on scheduled services was 69.4 per cent. By 1997 it was 71.9 per cent (Swissair, 2002a). The airline made an operating profit of $130 million on the back of improved productivity: '[T]he airline carried 22 per cent more passengers ... and wage costs fell from 32 per cent of total costs to 26 per cent' (Gill, 1998).

Despite these gains, politics and the market worked against the airline. Swissair was '... an airline suffering from restricted access to European Union routes due to Switzerland's non-EU status' says Gill. Swissair was also being outmanoeuvred on the international stage as other airlines forged alliances. Given that the purpose of an alliance is to cut costs through economies of scale,[30] Swissair feared it might get left behind. Consequently in 1995 Swissair took a stake in Sabena — a chronically unprofitable airline.

Oblivious, Swissair invested in other carriers with poor prospects, including Turkish Airlines (Turk Hava Yollari — THY), Polish Airlines (LOT), Air Portugal (TAP), Volare and the French regionals AOM, Air Liberté and Air Littoral. Swissair's strategy was simple: it '... bought stakes in loss-making airlines in the hope of turning them around' (*BBC News*, 2001d). In 1998 these unpromising enterprises coalesced into The *Quali*flyer Group.[31] Swissair, perhaps in denial, painted a determinedly rosy picture. Member airlines were '... committing themselves to top quality in all their products, services and activities'. They would deliver 'seamless customer care' through '... a unified quality standard anchored in excellence ... ' (Swissair, 2002a).

The plan was doomed. Fleck *et al.* (2001: 6-7) claim that Swissair '... went on an ill-conceived spending spree'. According to *The Economist* (2001b) Swissair took '... dubious minority stakes in a slew of wobbly European airlines'. Questions have been asked as to the quality of service offered by some of The *Quali*flyer Group's member airlines (Gill, 1998). It was not until 2006 that THY felt confident enough to approach airline grouping Star Alliance for membership. This may tell us something about that airline's health and Swissair's judgement when it was approached by the Swiss flag carrier in 1998. *Airliner World* (2006: 5) noted: '[THY] is unlikely to become a full member of the alliance until next summer at the earliest [i.e. summer 2007] as it must modify its business structures and activities to meet the group's stringent entry requirements'.

Schwarz (2002) talks of Swissair's 'forced expansion' which he attributes to an inflated corporate ego fuelled by an inflated national ego. As he explains: '[I]t was more a problem of this country's political culture than of Swissair's corporate culture, but the history of Swissair was, after all, also a reflection of the nation .... [T]he fundamental failing lay ... in Swissair's adamant determination to be one of the major players in international commercial aviation despite this country's modest size'. He attributes Swissair's 'much-bewailed hunter strategy' to 'overweaning ambition' and 'an almost pathological push to acquire holdings in other carriers'.

Despite a relatively good performance in 1997 Swissair's Chief Operating Officer Jeffrey Katz was under no illusions: 'This leadership dimension and competitiveness is what I'm working on ... at Swissair. Thinking about liberal and competitive situations is one of the biggest areas where the organisation [Swissair] needs to adjust ... ' (cited in Gill, 1998).

Nineteen ninety-seven was a watershed year for European aviation. On April 7th the EU's domestic aviation markets were deregulated. The resulting 'open skies' framework meant that any EU airline was 'free to operate domestic service[s] within the borders of any other member state'. In a March 24th, 1997 report AirWatch, a credit-rating agency, stated: 'Low-cost carriers will prevail'. AirWatch predicted deregulation's 'probable winners' to be BA, KLM, Lufthansa, SAS and Swiss Air Transport.

In 1998 Swissair suffered an aircraft loss. On September 2nd a McDonnell Douglas (now Boeing) MD-11 wide-bodied tri-jet operating service SWR111 from the US to Switzerland crashed into the sea off Nova Scotia killing 229 passengers and crew. The crew had reported smoke in the cockpit (Transportation Safety Board of Canada: 2001a). Given the airline's 'impeccable' safety record (Matthews, cited in Tran, 1998) the loss attracted attention. Swissair issued reassurances. SAirGroup's[32] Chief Executive Philippe Bruggisser stated: 'We believe that the aircraft was in impeccable technical condition when it left Geneva' (cited in Dowdney, 1998). SAirGroup's Chief Financial Officer claimed: 'This airplane was in perfect working order' (Schorderet, cited in Hopkins and Kettle, 1998). Swissair said it had no intention of withdrawing the type. When queried about the possibility that the fire had started in cockpit wiring, Bruggisser said that Swissair had pre-empted an airworthiness directive ordering that wires be insulated (Sage *et al.*, 1998). According to *BBC News* (1999): '[E]lectrical wiring recovered from the crash showed signs of arcing damage — a short circuit — similar to faults found in other MD-11s .... Key areas of damage discovered in the wreckage included a power feeding wire in an overhead circuit breaker and in the entertainment system'. In its final report the Transportation Safety Board of Canada (TSB) was a little more equivocal, stating that the arcing '... was likely associated with the fire initiation event; however, it could not be determined whether this arced wire was the lead event'. The TSB criticised Swissair's technical arm (SR Technics):

> While the SR Technics quality assurance (QA) programme design ... met required standards, the training and implementation process did not sufficiently ensure that the programme was consistently applied, so that potential safety aspects were always identified and mitigated (TSB, 2003).

On August 28, 2001 the TSB called for '... improved flammability standards for materials used in the pressurised portion of an aircraft'; '... a more stringent certification test regime for electrical wires'; and research and development work to '... reduce the potential for aircraft systems and sub-systems, such as ... oxygen supply lines, to worsen a fire in progress' (TSB, 2001b).

Although Swissair was largely exonerated by the TSB, Fleck *et al.* (2001: 6-7) describe the accident as Swissair's 'darkest moment'. 'It was a body blow for an airline with one of the best safety records in the world', they said.[33] On September 9th lawyers acting for one of the victims launched a £30 million lawsuit. There were complaints from fishermen that the rescue operation had prevented them from working. Swissair said it would think about compensation. Eventually Bruggisser was sacked.

In January 2001 Swissair abandoned its acquisitions policy. At a stormy March shareholders' meeting (attended by 10,000 or so) SAirGroup appointed Mario Corti, Nestlé's Chief Financial Officer, as Executive Chairman. Nine of Swissair's ten board members resigned, as did Swissair's CEO Moritz Suter. Suter had been in post less than two months.[34] SAirGroup attempted to revive morale announcing: 'This move lays the groundwork for a successful future that will focus on reviving the health of the company and, in particular, making Swissair again a top-quality and profitable airline' (*BBC News*, 2001a).

On April 2 2001 Corti announced a loss for 2000 of £1.2 billion. Over the year SAirGroup's share price had fallen by 45 per cent. The group described 2000 as 'the worst year in the history of the Swissair/SAirGroup'.[35] The huge loss became the subject of a criminal investigation. Hotel chain Swissotel was offered for sale. Towards the end of April the group announced it had secured a £408 million credit line from Deutsche Bank, CSFB and Citibank. In June 2001 rumours that Swissair was heading for bankruptcy caused the airline's share price to fall by over 13 per cent. According to *BBC News* (2001b): 'The rumours were sparked by a report in the *Financial Times* newspaper, which said that the airline is "facing a mounting bill to offload its loss-making French operations [AOM, Air Littoral and Air Liberté]"'. Swissair was indeed planning to withdraw from France. On June 5th the airline launched a recovery programme. 'Change 2001' aimed to cut costs. Staffing levels were to be reduced. The airline was helped by its pilots, who agreed to take a 5 per cent pay cut over the summer months. In a move designed to save money in the long term, SAirGroup agreed to pay Sabena £270 million in return for permission to withdraw from a commitment to increase its stake in the ailing flag carrier from 49.5 per cent to 85 per cent.[36]

In August Swissair announced its losses for the first half of the year: £98 million. Its debt burden was £6.25 billion. Urgent action was taken: 'In a desperate bid to reduce debt, Corti was forced to sell profitable subsidiaries, Swissport, the handling services, and Nuance Group airport retailers, and to cut flight capacity by 8%, with another 1,000 ground staff losing jobs, and 250 management positions facing the axe' (Fleck *et al.*, 2001: 6-7). SAirGroup hoped its divestments would raise £1.25 billion. This money was badly needed. Confidence was ebbing away. Between January and September Swissair's share price fell by about 80 per cent. Unable to ride out the post-September 11th downturn, on Tuesday October 2nd the airline grounded its aircraft. According to Swissair the country's two largest banks, UBS and Credit Suisse, had failed to meet a funding obligation. Without cash the airline could not pay airport and fuel charges. Aircraft were impounded across Europe. In Zurich, Swissair's base, the airline was refused fuel. The fleet lay idle for 48 hours until the Federal government stepped in. According to Fleck *et al.* (2001: 6-7) Switzerland was shaken:

> Switzerland is not a country that is given to panic. But the collapse of its national airline last week shook the nation to its core and plunged its business community into crisis .... In less than a week the collapse of Swissair inflicted more damage to the reputation of Swiss business than it has seen since the end of the second world war .... [Flag carriers have] enormous emotional attachments with their countries' people and governments.

According to *The Economist* (2001b) 'Such was [passengers'] incredulity at the grounding of the famous white-cross tailfin that many ... refused transfers ... '. The 'enormous emotional attachment' between the Swiss and Swissair was evidenced in media reporting of the collapse. The October 3rd editorial in the Swiss newspaper *Le Temps* ran: 'Even in the darkest hours of its history, the Soviet Aeroflot never appeared as pitiful as this. Is this company, shamefully immobilised on the tarmac, really the one which was the pride of generations of Swiss?' The newspaper was especially damning of UBS and Credit Suisse: 'How can the directors of the biggest banks in the country abandon the Swissair fleet without considering the damage inflicted to the national image?' The German-language tabloid *Blick* was more forthright:

> Everything we were proud of went to pot yesterday .... The white cross on red on the planes carried our reputation around the globe: it stood for quality and discipline. Since yesterday that's history. Worthless .... Switzerland ... is a banana republic.

The Swiss broadsheet *Neue Zürcher Zeitung* talked of 'massive damage': 'The pictures screened around the world of confiscated planes and planes grounded due to lack of fuel; the reports of stranded passengers ... will not only inflict massive damage on Swissair's image but on the whole of Switzerland' (cited in BBC News, 2001f). The *Tribune de Gèneve* spoke of national shame: 'It was almost too much .... To see the Swiss fleet nailed to the tarmac by debt — that was a big blow to Swiss pride. People felt ashamed, really ashamed. Even third world airlines don't take such a tumble' (Noel, cited in BBC News, 2001g). Sutton reported public anger: 'Firms like Swissair are a source of national pride. There is real anger in Switzerland towards the board ... ' (cited in Barter, 2001). Government and political figures spoke out. Johannes Matyassy, Director of Presence Switzerland, a federal promotions office, expressed his shock:

> Swissair, which carried our national flag, ensured the presence of Switzerland in many countries — and now that has disappeared .... It was unacceptable how we dealt with this crisis — to see the Swissair planes on the ground ... (cited in BBC News, 2001g)

The Swiss President, Moritz Leuenberger, deemed the airline's grounding 'unacceptable' (cited in BBC News, 2001e). Regarding UBS and Credit Suisse, the President professed himself 'profoundly disappointed in the behaviour of the banks'. Balz Hosly, President of the Swiss Office for Trade Expansion (OSEC) talked of '... the brutal grounding of the Swissair fleet' and alleged: '[T]he suspension of Swissair flights ... has done damage to Switzerland's image overseas' (Leuenberger and Hosly, cited in Swissinfo, 2001). Some years later journalist Peter Rothenbuler (cited in Foulkes, 2006) claimed a reflexive role for the collapse:

> [W]e thought Swissair was the best, we thought Switzerland was the best, we thought we were the best. We aren't, and it isn't. With Swissair, we found out it was rotten from the inside. Now we're wondering if a lot of other things are rotten from the inside.

Rothenbuler suggests that corporate behaviour can provide insights into national psyches. Following the grounding a protest march was organised. Ten thousand marched through Zurich's financial district protesting the behaviour of UBS and Credit Suisse. Mario Corti blamed the two banks for Swissair's embarrassing and costly 48-hour grounding. In a *swissinfo* report dated October 4th, 2001 Urs Ackermann, a spokesman for the Zurich Cantonal Bank, alleged 'a growing number of UBS customers' were 'closing their accounts following the bank's dealings with Swissair'. Ackermann claimed: 'Our new customers are telling us they feel personally wounded that their banks were unable to come up with a solution for the embattled Swissair' (cited in Zarifeh, 2001). The *TagesAnzeiger* newspaper accused the banks of humiliating the Federal government. *Neue Zürcher Zeitung* accused UBS and Credit Suisse of undermining 'trust in our economic system' and of damaging 'the reputation of Switzerland' and 'the Swiss airline industry'. Switzerland's political parties also rounded on the banks (Zarifeh, 2001).

The demonisation of UBS and Credit Suisse reflected the popular view that the banks should have acted in the national interest. That is, they should have put Swissair's financial security before their own. In the midst of an orgy of Swiss nationalism the public forgot that the banks' *only* obligation was to generate profit and dividend. In their constitution and operation UBS and Credit Suisse were not 'public corporations'.[37] In the swirl of emotions following Swissair's collapse this vital fact was forgotten.

The Swiss government moved to stabilise Swissair, providing sufficient cash for the airline to re-start operations. *The Economist* (2001b) attributed this largesse to 'public pressure'. Schwarz (2002) has since put the view that Swissair failed because of 'selective perception'. '[A] crass gap [developed] between our self-image and the world's image of us' he says. 'This loss of the sense of reality affected pilots and other Swissair personnel, the enterprise's top management, influential business and political figures and sometimes the entire country'. In other words, says Schwarz, the origins of Swissair's demise lay partly in its own hubris and lack of objectivity. 'Autosuggestion — the cavalier overlooking of weaknesses and criticism — is no formula for success'.

Towards the end of October 2001 a rescue package was announced. Under the scheme the Swiss federal government would take a 20 per cent stake in the 'new' Swissair. Swiss regional governments would take an 18 per cent stake and private enterprise 62 per cent (Barker, 2001). According to an editorial in the *Financial Times* the Swiss government saved its national airline by '... finding others to do it for them'. Done and Dombey (2001) concur: '[I]n Switzerland emotional appeals have been made to large companies to save the national airline .... More than half the companies in the Swiss Market Index of blue-chip stocks are investing more than SFr1.5bn (£620m) of shareholders' funds to try to retain a national airline'.

At the beginning of November 2001 it was announced that the 'new' Swissair would provide both European *and* intercontinental services, but with the new carrier '... being rebuilt around the lower cost structure of Crossair [Swissair's original 'low cost' regional carrier]'. Some believed the plan to be 'far too ambitious given Switzerland's relatively small size' (Hall and Bickerton, 2001). Rainer Gut, chair of the public/private committee tasked with overseeing the initiative, disagreed: '[T]he captains of Swiss industry, led by Mr Gut, have made it very clear that Switzerland needs much more than a regional European airline' (Hall and Bickerton, 2001). Clearly the government, industry and public were determined to resurrect their flag carrier. By mid-December 2001 it appeared that the ambition might be realised. In a December 18th press release Swissair announced that by December 15th its load factor had increased to 75 per cent: 'It was the first time since the grounding that the load factor exceeded last year's figure' (Swissair, 2001).

In January 2002 the electors of Canton Zurich voted to invest in the 'new Swissair'. According to a press release from SAirGroup (Swissair, 2002c): 'The result is a clear acknowledgement of the vital role played by this key component in the country's public transport system, in both social and economic terms'. The Swiss, through the ballot box, had once again demonstrated their affection for the airline-as-totem concept. The new totem would be known as Swiss International Air Lines (or just 'Swiss'). The airline's political origins have been acknowledged by Swiss's CEO, André Dosé. 'The new airline is a unique instance ... of a collective alliance of politics, industry and the people of Switzerland' he said in January 2002 (cited in Swiss, 2002a).

5.3 Swiss: a new beginning

The new airline had numerous problems to overcome. Like Pan Am in its death throes it had a poor image. Husband (2002) observed of a Crossair service: '[Their] dowdy Heathrow lounge has run out of wine glasses. Yellowing Monet prints dot the walls. The economy cabin is uncomfortably cramped'. In January 2002 Swiss International Air Lines's agency, Wink Media, explained its marketing strategy. Wink's Tyler Brûlé said Swiss would cultivate (or recultivate) an image of style and relative exclusivity. Its buzzwords would be 'comfort', 'civilised' and 'global'. The Swiss, said Brûlé, had recovered their national carrier:

We want this airline to sell Switzerland to the world .... We need to reinvent the whole culture of air travel, and we're going to do it ... with a combination of elegance and understatement .... It will be aspirational .... It will be elite .... [T]his is a real opportunity to bring romance and glamour back .... We're not looking for the typical Ryanair passenger [sic] (cited in Husband, 2002).

By February 2002 the new airline's size, shape and operational regime had been decided. New, more economic aircraft types were ordered, including the Embraer 170 and 195 models and Airbus A340-300 (Campbell, 2002b). Former Swissair pilots hired by Swiss agreed to a 35 per cent wage cut. Unit costs on international routes were to be cut by 15 per cent and on European routes by 7 per cent. To this end leasing charges were reduced by between 30 and 40 per cent in comparison to those paid by Swissair. Referring to cost savings André Dosé commented: 'With a strong future potential and lower cost base [than Swissair] the chances are good for breaking even in 2003' (cited in Penney, 2002: 58).[38]

On March 27, 2002 Crossair officially became Swiss International Air Lines. Penney (2002: 56) says the airline's ownership on this date was distributed between the business sector, institutional investors, the Swiss government, the Zurich government, Switzerland's banks and other Swiss regional authorities. Swiss, said *Flight International*, intended 'to become Europe's fourth largest airline'. André Dosé wanted his airline to be 'best in class'. To that end Dosé raised about £1.64 billion. On their tails Swiss's aircraft carried a large white cross on a red ground (Gill, 2002). Penney (2002: 58) says Swiss's 'brand personality' reflected 'such long-held Swiss values as top quality service, punctuality, reliability, attention to detail, tradition and cosmopolitan elegance'. In May 2002 Pinkham (2002: 43) described Swiss as 'the new national flag carrier'.

Swissair's transmutation confirmed Campbell's (2002a) prediction: 'In the case of flag carriers especially, it is likely that European governments ...

will try to set up successor airlines — often struggling with ... an undersized domestic market [in Switzerland's case roughly seven million people]'. What happened in Switzerland was not unique. On the other side of the globe the New Zealand government took Air New Zealand back into public ownership 12 years after the flag carrier had been privatised. According to *Flight International* (2002a) the airline was re-nationalised for strategic reasons: 'Wellington's reasoning is that a small, isolated country ... with a scattered population, needs a domestic air transport infrastructure and connections with the world'. The New Zealand Government believed that only it could ensure the security of the country's transport infrastructure.

The 1990s, claims Heywood (1998: 60-62), saw the rise of 'neo-Keynesianism'[39] which 'developed out of the failure of the free market revolution of the 1980s to reverse long-term economic decline', and the realisation that 'unregulated capitalism tends to bring low investment [and] short-termism'. Both the Swiss and New Zealand governments made Keynesian interventions to resurrect their national carriers. *The Economist* (2001c) stated: '[T]hese cases suggest that Europe is back to its old tricks, doling out generous subsidies to "strategic" companies'.[40] Given that Swiss adopted Crossair's cost structure (Crossair's flight and cabin crew were paid 35 per cent and 10 per cent less than their Swissair colleagues) it is fair to say that the rescue package was a mix of 'old tricks' and 'new realism' (Hall and Odell, 2002).

5.4 Lufthansa-Swiss: a new beginning revisited
Unfortunately for its employees and passengers, neo-Keynesianism did not save Swiss International Air Lines. In 2002 the airline lost nearly one thousand million francs. In 2003 it halved its order for new, ultra-efficient Embraer 170 regional twin-jets.[41] By June 2003 it was losing £900,000 each day. It decided to reduce its fleet size by nearly a third and shed more jobs. The markets were unimpressed: in 2003 the company's share value fell by 60 per cent. To steady nerves the company issued a statement: 'The

enduring crisis in the airline industry points to sector-wide consolidation. Only healthy, well-positioned companies will survive' (cited in *BBC News*, 2003b).

In November 2004 the airline's Chief Executive warned that he saw 'a rocky road' ahead and that the airline must 'significantly reduce costs' (Franz, cited in *BBC News*, 2004). In the summer of 2005 Swiss International Air Lines finally accepted reality: it agreed to a takeover by Lufthansa. The Swiss no longer had an independent flying totem — although as Phillips (2005) explains the airline was to be more than just an appendage of the Teutonic titan:

> Air France controls KLM, and Lufthansa ... Swiss, but in both cases the targets are maintaining their national identities and operations because the countries made that a condition of any deal .... In the case of both Swiss and KLM, the airlines not only must keep their identities but also must maintain a major hub operation in each country.

Despite the takeover Swiss's rhetoric was unchanged: 'No airline is more Swiss than SWISS. For our customers, this means such classic Swiss values as quality, reliability and hospitality' (2006). When Lufthansa bought Swiss International Air Lines, the airline's President and CEO, Christoph Franz, stated: 'With Lufthansa and SWISS, we are seeing the team-up of two globally-reputed airlines with the same strong commitment to *superior service and quality* (emphasis added)' (cited in Deutsche Lufthansa AG, 2005). Clearly airline executives' self perceptions are highly resilient.

6 Case study 3: Sabena

6.1 Sabena — a short history

Sabena's bankruptcy was a blow to Europe's proud aviation tradition. Founded in 1923, Belgium's Societé Anonyme Belge d'Exploitation de la Navigation Aérienne (Belgian Company for the Exploitation of Air

Navigation) pioneered air routes to Europe's capital cities (it was the first airline to operate scheduled helicopter services to major European cities) and Belgium's colonies (like the Congo). Europe's second-oldest airline was not a money-spinner, however. Indeed the airline only once made a profit after 1958. Like Pan Am, Sabena struggled to compete in the 1980s. In 1995 Swissair took a 49.5 per cent stake in Sabena, which was by then a private limited company. The government held 50.5 per cent.

In 2000, with a load factor of 61.2 per cent, Sabena made the largest loss in its history. The airline's CEO outlined Sabena's several problems: 'Costs have overtaken revenue mainly because of the rising cost of fuel, the unfavourable dollar exchange rate, low yield, too many economy passengers, insufficient load factors and overcapacity on too many destinations' (Müeller, cited in De Wulf, 2002). A full 82.4 per cent of the airline's passengers flew low-yield Economy. This was disastrous for a high-cost legacy carrier like Sabena. The Belgian Parliament debated the airline's plight.

In 2001 Sabena's CEO drew attention to what he believed to be his airline's chief problem — its inflated self-image. As he put it, Sabena needed to 'get modest again' (Müeller, cited in *BBC News*, 2001c). A rescue plan was put forward. It included: a commitment by the Belgian government and Swissair to improve the carrier's finances; the loss of 1,600 jobs; the release of aircraft; a focus on high-yield passengers (i.e. businesspeople); the axing of loss-making routes to Beirut, Belfast, Catania, Faro, Verona, Washington and Tokyo; and the sale of Sabena's maintenance, cargo-handling and catering arms, its information technology operation Atraxis, the Sabena Flight Academy, the airline's charter arm Sobelair and its hotel interests.[42] According to the CEO: 'Without this plan there is no survival, we will go straight to concordat [bankruptcy protection]' (Müeller, cited in *BBC News*, 2001c). Sabena's employees responded by striking. In the week beginning August 5th Sabena cancelled 150 flights.

Sabena filed for bankruptcy protection in October 2001. A plan to cut 2,000 out of 12,000 jobs was opposed by Sabena's pilots (represented by the Belgian Cockpit Association (BCA)). In a subsequent referendum, however, 57 per cent of Sabena's employees voted in favour of the CEO's restructuring plan, outflanking the BCA. The weeks following the September 11th attacks saw the emergence of a new aviation industry *realpolitik* — a realisation that Europe's legacy carriers had been living on borrowed time (Barter, 2001). Given that Sabena had made a profit on only two occasions it is possible that the airline, opposed from without and within and with enormous structural problems, would have failed even without September 11th. Although long in the offing, Sabena's failure still shocked Belgium's Prime Minister, who described the airline's collapse as 'a moment of impotence and failure' (Verhofstadt, cited in Dombey, 2001: 23). The country's Transport Minister said: 'It is very important for the people on a national level to have a national company, not only for the people who work and who [now] don't have a job' (Durant, cited in *BBC News*, 2001h). Belgium's Employment Minister described the collapse as 'an economic and social disaster' (Onkelinx, cited in *BBC News*, 2001h). A Sabena Passenger Services Assistant observed: 'The country is down. It's finished with Sabena' (Ronald op de Beeck, cited in *BBC News*, 2001h). Castle (2001) observed: 'For the Belgian government the demise of its flag carrier is a political humiliation'.

6.2 SN: a new beginning
In 2002 Delta Air Transport, Sabena's regional arm, became SN Brussels Airlines, the 'new' Sabena. Overseen by SN Air Holding, SN Brussels operated 32 four-engine Avro Regional Jets, to which it added a small number of Airbus short and long-range aircraft. Despite operating a mixed fleet, delivering a full-service product and running its own maintenance operation, SN Brussels made profits in 2003, 2004 and 2005, something its predecessor had found difficult. Of course, SN Brussels had one very important advantage over its predecessor — unlike Sabena it was not an

instrument or slave of government. Flag carriers like Sabena had little room for manoeuvre. In November 2001 Sabena's Chairman offered this analysis of the problem: '[Sabena] had to be a flag carrier and therefore had to do things which basically couldn't earn any money' (Chaffart, cited in *BBC News*, 2001h).

6.3 SN-Virgin Express: a new beginning revisited
'Nobody at Sabena would do the same thing with Virgin Express again. This contract has not been very beneficial for us, either on the financial or customer side' (Müeller, cited in *Flight International*, 2001a). So said Sabena's CEO of his airline's business arrangement with Virgin Express in August 2001. In April 2005 SB Brussels and Virgin Express were put under the common ownership of SN Airholding. It seemed that Belgium's aviation industry was being rationalised for the long term. Merger talks were first held in December 2001.

In the next section the data and opinion presented above with respect to Pan Am, Swissair and Sabena is analysed with reference to the academic theory described at the beginning of this paper. In an effort to understand their chronic demise Section 7 evaluates how closely Pan Am, Swissair and Sabena approximated Pauchant and Mitroff's model of the 'crisis-prone' organisation.

7 Discussion
7.1 Pan Am
Having failed to come to terms with the new economic realities of deregulation Pan Am staggered on in a weakened state until overcome by events. Sipika and Smith characterise Pan Am's demise as a 'chronic slow erosion' with the airline porpoising between contiguous 'defensive turnaround positions' and periods of consolidation (1992: 21-28).

Pan Am was a crisis-prone corporation. Despite the advent of Reaganomics, Pan Am pilots assumed their airline would be rescued (denial and disavowal). Having enjoyed a half-century of government patronage and institutional protection Pan Am employees developed feelings of 'omnipotence, perfection and all-powerfulness'. If Gandt is correct these sentiments survived to the bitter end (grandiosity). Employees conjured up 'feelings of omnipotence' through their lionisation of Pan Am's charismatic founder and long-serving CEO (idealisation). Finally Pan Am's numerous technological and operational innovations and several 'firsts' (like the first 747 service) would have reinforced employees' feelings of 'omnipotence, perfection and all-powerfulness'. (Pan Am innovated after deregulation, too).

Pan Am's policy of selling the family silver and of ducking the market trend for merger evidenced 'fixation'. (Only when staring into the abyss of bankruptcy did management consider alliances).[43] Pan Am sold its promising Pacific Division, leaving it with just the volatile North Atlantic market.[44] The pace and scope of divestment was dizzying. According to Robinson: 'Pan Am ... sold almost as many assets in 14 months as Trippe had ... built ... over the previous 50 years'. Robinson (1994: 173-176) also asserts: 'Had Pan Am been more aggressive in offering itself as a merger candidate ... [the airline] would have been put in a stronger position ... '. Unfortunately for Pan Am's employees the airline's managers had fixed on a business model — a slimmed-down but still independent carrier — that stood little chance of success. The fixation on slimming-down produced some questionable decisions: Plaskett's sale of Pan Am World Services, a wholly-owned subsidiary that was grossing about $500 million a year, was foolhardy.

Pan Am's poor service levels add more weight to the view that it was not a 'positive self-regard corporation' but a 'self-inflated corporation' (although Plaskett did address this issue during the late 1980s). Before Plaskett customers were regarded as a means to an end. Acker's feud with Shugrue absorbed energies that should have been focused on passengers. This behaviour again matches Mitroff *et al.*'s (1989: 274) description of the crisis-prone organisation – one that is possessed of an 'unhealthy narcissism'. Plaskett's mishandling of the public relations aspects of the Lockerbie disaster is further evidence of Pan Am's 'self-inflated corporation' status. His bunker mentality reflected and reproduced a corporate culture that encouraged introversion and self-obsession. If Pan Am had been a 'positive self-regard corporation' Plaskett would, like British Midland Chairman Sir Michael Bishop in the immediate aftermath of the Kegworth disaster, have hastened to the disaster scene. According to David, Bishop's timely action enabled British Midland to manage a situation 'which could have inflicted considerable damage on its reputation' (cited in Smith, 1992: 63). (In Sipika and Smith's language, while Bishop successfully handled the media dimension of his disaster's 'Defensive Phase', Plaskett did not). Two years before Lockerbie Pan Am had been told by Israeli consultants that its security at several European gateway airports was 'dangerously lax'. Believing the findings to be 'too harsh' Pan Am's security chief dismissed the consultants (Bremner, 1988). This behaviour evidenced both 'disavowal' and 'denial' on the part of Pan Am's management, especially as 'Aviation terrorism began to surface, for the first time on any major scale, *in Europe* in the summer of 1985 (emphasis added)' (Robinson, 1994: 177).

Certain assumptions, or, in Mitroff and Pauchant's language 'fallacies', persisted after Trippe's departure and the CAB's abolition:

'The fallacy of protection/resource abundance' — even in the midst of crisis Pan Am's pilots did not believe the government would let the company fail (in the same way that Pan Am's pilots did not believe the government would allow Eastern to fail).

'The fallacy of size' — Pan Am had been 'the world's largest and most profitable airline' (Robinson, 1994: ix). Until deregulation Pan Am had only one serious US rival on international routes, TWA. In the 1980s Pan Am still had a sizeable workforce, fleet and network. At the time of

Lockerbie the airline had 126 aircraft, including thirty-eight 747s. (TWA had nineteen). Also, and perhaps most crucially, under Trippe's tutelage Pan Am had become an institution. Even after Acker and Plaskett exposed the 'imperial airline' to economic reality, many Pan Am pilots clung to the old imperial mindset. To paraphrase Mitroff and Pauchant: 'They had grown up and lived most of their existence in a regulated or quasi-regulated environment'. To the extent that Pan Am's glorious past and their own institutionalisation led them to redefine the new reality *in their own terms*, Pan Am's pilots compounded the carrier's difficulties. Pauchant and Mitroff (1988: 58) put it this way: '[T]he SIC group redefines reality to suit its fantasies and beliefs about itself .... [T]his misperception of reality is not motivated primarily by *rational* blocks ... but rather through *emotional* blocks ... [employees] not having the *emotional resources* to face up to critical situations'.

But employees' behaviour was never *exclusively* SIC. At the same time pilots were expecting the government to save Pan Am (a belief partly born of sentiment) they were offering salary cuts (a practical contribution). Indeed the entire workforce made sacrifices. They resented the sale of the Pacific Division. They protested against management 'incompetence'. Certainly they feared unemployment. But they also feared for an American institution (PSRC-type behaviour). Like their staff, Acker and Plaskett indulged in both SIC and PSRC-type behaviour. Acker's feud with Shugrue and decision to return to a mixed fleet, and Plaskett's post-Lockerbie recalcitrance, were SIC-type behaviours. The evidence suggests:

a) that Acker's mixed fleet was economically foolhardy;[45]

b) that his feud with Marty Shugrue was distracting; and

c) that Plaskett's recalcitrance was a public relations disaster with serious consequences for Pan Am's image, sales and, ultimately, chances of recovery.

On the basis of the analysis presented here it is clear that Pan Am displayed several of the characteristics of Pauchant and Mitroff's crisis-prone organisation. At various times and to varying degrees Pan Am employees indulged in denial, disavowal and fixation. The beliefs and expectations that constituted the airline's 'core' left it with, to use Pauchant and Mitroff's (1992: 49) phrase, 'Plans, Mechanisms and Procedures for Crisis Management' inadequate to the task.

Pan Am's core was not *entirely* rotten, however. The workforce made sacrifices, believed in Pan Am the institution and, initially at least, supported Acker. As for Acker and Plaskett, they helped and hindered Pan Am. The emphasis on quality was a positive. The ill-advised purchases (National) and sales (Pan Am World Services and the Pacific Division) were a negative. The failure to integrate National drained the airline. The abuse of snapback alienated staff. Management's antipathy to competitive tendering proved costly. Senior managers feuded. Lockerbie was mismanaged. Applying Pauchant and Mitroff's onion model to Pan Am it can be seen that the 'Character of the Individuals Working for the Organisation'[46] was an admixture of selfishness, sacrifice, skill and incompetence. Pan Am's core was a paradox of positives and negatives. There is evidence that the airline's core was composed of various 'deep beliefs and defensive mechanisms', including disavowal, grandiosity and idealisation. These cultural attributes were inimical to crisis management.

Perhaps the most interesting question is *how* these beliefs persisted a) after Trippe's retirement and the CAB's abolition and b) through Acker and Plaskett's hard-headed regimes. Could it be that corporations with a tradition of service to and patronage by the state are possessed of a near-immutable world-view that is simply handed, unmodified, from one generation of employee to the next (and which is reproduced for public consumption (and future employees) by the media)? Pauchant and Mitroff (1988: 54) assert: '[C]ulture is to an organisation what personality is to an individual'. Pan Am's staff retained their (dysfunctional) 'imperial' mindset to the end. Pan Am's personality transcended deregulation and defied manipulation.

7.2 Swissair/Swiss International Air Lines/Lufthansa-Swiss
Swissair had much in common with Pan Am. Both airlines were flag carriers (Swissair formally and Pan Am tacitly). Both benefited from state investment: Swissair directly, Pan Am more subtly through US Mail and other government contracts. Both suffered major air disasters a couple of years before their demise. Pan Am's was Lockerbie. Swissair's was SWR111. (Crossair also suffered a loss in January 2000 and another in November 2001).[47] The *coup de grace* for both airlines was a major event with global social, economic and political repercussions. In the case of Pan Am it was the Gulf War. In the case of Swissair, the attacks of September 11th, 2001. Both airlines had long-term financial problems. Both Pan Am and Swissair revamped their product. Both emphasised (or re-emphasised) quality. Both made acquisitions, then, when their respective prospects worsened, divestments (both sold their in-house hotel chains). Both invested in unsuitable airlines (like National and Sabena). Both experienced boardroom strife. Given these similarities Toft's theory of isomorphic learning suggests that Swissair could have learned much from Pan Am.

In terms of Mitroff and Pauchant's taxonomy, Swissair's high standards of customer care placed it in the PSRC category. The airline courted high-spending (and therefore high-margin) travellers with a premium product. To sustain this 'outward-looking' policy it spent heavily on staffing and other aspects of customer care. As with BA, Swissair's reliance on the wealthy traveller made it vulnerable to fluctuations in the luxury/business market. When, after September 11th, traffic on the North Atlantic declined[48] carriers like Swissair (and BA) suffered disproportionately.

The fact that Swissair acted to help those affected by the SWR111 crash (from passengers' relatives to Nova Scotia fishermen) is further evidence of its PSRC credentials. It also made positive moves on the technical front. On August 5th, 1999 SAirGroup and Boeing concluded an agreement that would, according to the airline, '[accelerate] the process of settling damage claims and [enable] swift compensation of family members in cases of proven damage' (Swissair, 1999).

While Swissair's focus on customer care was a PSRC-type behaviour its global ambitions produced SIC-type behaviour. Unfortunately for Swissair its SIC-type behaviour (its large investments in *Quali*flyer airlines) blinded it to several unpalatable facts: First, Swissair's small home market of about seven million people was too small to support a global player; secondly, other flag carriers had stolen a march on Swissair. They were already in alliances. Consequently Swissair was always chasing the game; thirdly, as a result of its tardiness Swissair's choice of partner airlines was limited. Certain airlines (THY and LOT, for example) could not (initially) offer the level of service that had become Swissair's trademark. Given the nature of codeshare arrangements (where a Swissair ticket-holder might find her/himself on a THY flight, for example) Swissair's image may have suffered through its operational associations. Lastly, Swissair invested in airlines with dubious financial records (Sabena, for example).

When their decisions were queried Swissair managers employed the defensive mechanisms of the SIC corporation. Jeffrey Katz, Swissair's Chief Operating Officer, observed: 'Sabena is well on track. It has many more things that it desires to do on the marketing, product and cost sides. And those [plans] really seem to be moving well' (cited in Gill, 1998). Given Sabena's record up to the date of Katz's assertion (July, 1998) it could be argued that he was guilty of both denial and fixation. The former because of Sabena's inability to make money and the latter because of his determination to keep Sabena in the *Quali*flyer group. It is a matter of record that Sabena struggled right up to its bankruptcy in the first week of November 2001. At the beginning of August 2001 Sabena announced significant redundancies. It had lost £86.9 million in the first half of 2001.

In response the Belgian Government (which owned 50.5 per cent of the company) and Swissair (which owned the rest) agreed to invest more money in the airline. On hearing of the redundancies Sabena employees struck. In the week commencing August 5th the airline cancelled 150 flights (BBC News, 2001d). On the day it failed Sabena owed £1.4 billion. Clearly Katz's 1998 prognosis was wrong (although he is being judged with the benefit of hindsight).

As to Swissair's organisational culture, in 1998 Katz observed: 'Thinking about liberal and competitive situations is one of the biggest areas where the organisation [Swissair] needs to adjust ... ' (cited in Gill, 1998). It is interesting to ponder why Swissair thought it could pay its flight and cabin crew so much. While high remunerations accorded with the airline's business model of a metronomic airline delivering high-quality service to high-paying clients headed for prestige destinations, they were unsustainable. Perhaps staff thought the airline's totemism guaranteed survival? It is possible that Swissair staff were also influenced by what was happening industry-wide. According to *The Economist* (2001c) flag carriers like Air France, Iberia and Olympic benefited from '[an] endless round of hand-outs' from their national governments. Given that, as Mitroff and Pauchant put it, a company's outlook is (partly) a function of 'the context in which [it] competes' and 'the structure of its industry', Swissair was simply following industry fashion. The industry's dependency culture was irresistible. In the same way that a child who grows up on an ugly, amenity-less, crime-ridden sink estate is impacted by her/his environment, Swissair succumbed to its milieu.

Katz was right to focus on cost-efficiency. In April 2001 SAirGroup announced a loss of £1.2 billion for the previous year. According to SAirGroup 2000 was '[T]he worst year in the history of the Swissair/SAirGroup'. A criminal investigation was launched and Swissotel was put on the market (echoing Pan Am's sale of InterContinental). Following the President of Switzerland's description of Swissair's grounding as 'unacceptable' the Swiss government engineered a pared-down replacement — Swiss. Politically the government had no choice but to engineer a replacement: 'The 2001 bankruptcy of Swissair, a national icon, weighed heavily on the country when it was on the verge of sliding into economic malaise ... the gold-standard carrier was replaced within a short time by a smaller airline named Swiss' (Phillips, 2005). While Swiss was different in kind to Swissair it was still seen as Switzerland's flag carrier. As such Swiss, like Swissair, may well have developed feelings of 'omnipotence, perfection and all-powerfulness'.

Swissair's organisational culture was something of a curate's egg. On the one hand, as with its emphasis on passenger comfort, it fell within the PSRC camp. On the other, as with its *Quali*flyer initiative, it was a classic SIC corporation — grandiose and myopic. Sometimes both forms of behaviour manifested simultaneously — as with its post-SWR111 actions. At the same time Swissair was caring for victims' families (archetypal PSRC behaviour) its senior managers were making claims that were, to say the least, precipitous. SAirGroup's Chief Executive asserted: 'We believe ... the aircraft was in impeccable technical condition ... '. His Chief Financial Officer said: 'This airplane was in perfect working order'. (As most engineers would confirm it is unwise to use adjectives like 'impeccable' and 'perfect' when describing complex machinery). Although subsequent investigations confirmed the airworthiness of the MD-11 there is no way that SAirGroup's managers could have been certain of the facts at the time they made their statements. To the extent that their assertions evidenced feelings of 'omnipotence' and 'perfection' both SAirGroup's CEO and Chief Financial Officer were guilty of 'grandiosity' — a behaviour characteristic of employees of SIC corporations.

7.3 Sabena/SN/SN-Virgin Express
Sabena suffered from many of the problems that afflicted Pan Am and Swissair. The most fundamental of Sabena's problems was its role as

Belgium's aerial ambassador. Like all flag carriers, Sabena did things that a market-focused, privately-owned airline would never have done, like operating unprofitable services to far-flung capital cities, often of Belgium's ex-colonies. It became bloated. On the day of its bankruptcy the airline, which had made a profit on only two occasions, employed 11,463 staff. Sabena's successor airline, the non-flag carrying SN Brussels, made a profit in successive years with 2,367 staff. Despite its small establishment SN operated to 55 European and 14 African destinations.

During Sabena's last days some of its staff displayed SIC-type behaviour. In response to Sabena's rescue plan, its pilots called for strike action. The airline's final days witnessed wildcat strikes by several employee groups, including luggage, cleaning, catering and check-in staff. According to Castle (2001: 17): 'Those [passengers] who tried to call the airline were greeted with a recorded message ... saying that the office was closed because of industrial action'. Over the years, Sabena had seen a good deal of labour unrest, an indication that many staff cared 'only or mainly about themselves'.

In the changed market conditions of the deregulated 1990s Sabena was a 'dinosaur' airline. Its refusal or inability to change sealed its fate. The closing months of 2001 witnessed the start of the long-awaited shake-out of Europe's civil aviation industry. As a Swiss analyst observed in October 2001: 'There are simply too many airlines around — about a third will have to go' (Moser, cited in Barter, 2001).

8 Conclusion

This analysis suggests that Pan Am, Swissair and Sabena were self-inflated corporations and therefore 'crisis-prone'. Characteristics like 'grandiosity' and 'denial' may not be uncommon amongst airlines, however. For years airlines like BA and BMI British Midland eschewed the 'low-cost' business model. They did not consider carriers like easyJet (which launched in 1995 on another carrier's AOC) to be a threat. In response to the runaway success of Ryanair and easyJet, BA and BMI adopted elements of the low-cost business model (like one-way fares, no-service sectors (i.e. no free meals or drinks) and on-line bookings) (*Flight International*, 2002d: 7). Both launched low-cost subsidiaries.

On his retirement as IATA Director General in June 2002, Pierre Jeanniot accused the airline industry of collective myopia: 'We simply cannot blame all our poor results on external factors .... [T]his industry was ill-prepared to successfully weather even a fairly mild, regular economic cycle. When a business is concentrating on market growth the focus is seldom on costs' (cited in Ionides, 2002: 21). The reaction of BA's pilots to their company's efforts to cut costs (in order to survive) was an example of 'collective myopia'. Following BA's economic nosedive after September 11th Rod Eddington, the company's CEO, aimed to reduce the workforce by 23 per cent (some 13,000 jobs) and to freeze wages until 2003. John Frohnsdorff of the British Air Line Pilots' Association warned: 'We will step up our efforts to prevent any airline taking unfair advantage of the aftermath of September 11 to cut pilot jobs, or use it as an excuse to reduce pay and benefits or working conditions' (cited in Odell, 2002). According to Odell: '[In June 2002] senior BA union activists were ... talking up the possibility of "a strike by Christmas"' (Odell, 2002). Such behaviour was not unlike the response of Pan Am's unions to Acker and Plaskett's efforts to thin down Pan Am (although the 'snapback' episode did annoy Pan Am staff) and the reaction of Sabena's employees to attempts to save the flag carrier. In Sabena's case there was labour unrest both before September 11th and after. In February 2001, for example, Sabena's flight crew staged an unofficial strike 'causing the cancellation of two-thirds of all flights and pushing the airline to the brink of collapse'. In August 2001 'Sabena was forced to cancel two-thirds of its services after some 350 ground workers staged an unofficial walk-out in protest at the leaking of the carrier's long-awaited business plan' (*FT.com*, 2002). Clearly these staff were interested more in their own circumstances than those of Sabena's customers. This was SIC-type behaviour.

The Swiss reincarnated Swissair with Swiss International Air lines. While Swiss's business model was different in some respects, the airline continued Swissair's policy of offering a premium product to the discerning customer. Swiss's buzzwords were similar to those used by Swissair ('top quality'; a standard of service 'anchored in excellence') . Campbell (2002b) stated: 'With other airlines [like BA and BMI British Midland] adopting elements of the successful low-cost strategy Swiss stands out. It plans to improve inflight services and increase seat-pitch in all classes ...'.

Swiss (2002a) promised to trade on 'quality', 'elegance' and 'perfect service'. The airline was launched on Easter Sunday 2002 under the slogan 'The return of civilised aviation'. Its CEO André Dosé was unconcerned about competition from low-cost carriers: 'We have a certain competition on some routes from easyJet but overall our market wants a high-quality product' (cited in *BBC News*, 2002). While the Swiss government has made it difficult for non-Swiss airlines to operate in Switzerland restrictive practices may, in time, be swept away by the forces of globalisation and free trade.

It is interesting to ponder whether Swiss's pursuit of the 'aspirational' reflected a cool-headed business calculation or just a sentimental attachment to its predecessor's values. Were the new CEO and board unduly influenced by Swissair's lustrous history and the Swiss public's penchant for quality? A business plan determined by hubris and national fervour rather than calculation is a disaster-in-waiting. As Campbell (2002b) noted at the time: '... Swiss will be going against the trend if it can make a high-quality service profitable ... '.[49]

Swiss was not alone in trying to 'buck the market'. According to *Flight International* it was business-as-usual for both Air France and Lufthansa. Air France's chairman stated: 'I am often asked: Does Air France feel threatened by [low cost operators?] .... We are not in the same business. The flexibility, service and frequencies offered by major carriers cannot be compared with what low-cost airlines have to offer' (Spinetta, cited in Campbell and Kingsley-Jones, 2002: 38). Rattray (cited in Pilling, 2002) noted: 'The low-cost road is ... not the only one. There is still a very significant tranche of people who want to be called Sir'.[50] Speaking in November 2001 Ryanair's CEO exclaimed: 'The Swiss would have laughed at us two months ago, some Paddy airline offering cheap fares, but not any longer' (O'Leary, cited in Osborne, 2001).[51] *Flight International* (2002c) observed: '[I]nertia, myopia and delusional overconfidence ... [will cause] great and unnecessary suffering for the European flag carriers'. Calder (2002b) ventured: 'Some people in the airline business have yet to grasp that what they are selling is not the pleasure of sitting in an aluminium tube ....We are buying ... the smile of a loved one realising that the distance between them and you has diminished'. (One might suggest that in an industry where the only certainty is uncertainty (Bennett, 2006) *all* airlines, whether flag-carrying or low-cost, should guard against over-confidence).

Latest (2006) figures suggest that the full-service model is in retreat: 'Eurocontrol ... states that in the past 12 months, low-cost carriers added 2.4 percentage points to their market share ... this growth is equivalent to 83% of all net additional flights, illustrating that little growth was achieved by the legacy carriers' (Endres, 2006: 21). In August 2006 Field wrote: 'Globally, the low-fares sector provided 16% of capacity in July [2006] — double its 8% share just five years earlier .... In the USA, their market share is 26% — up from 18% five years ago' (2006b: 13). In their pursuit of market dominance and maximum profit low-cost carriers like Ryanair are prepared to go to law (Baker, 2006a: 20; Barrow, 2006: 4).[52] This is indicative of their determination to annihilate the opposition — especially Europe's remaining legacy carriers. This determination can sometimes rebound on LCCs, however. According to Granshaw (2006: 2) in 2006 a Dublin court hearing a case brought by Ryanair against the Ryanair

European Pilots' Association accused the airline's executives of giving 'false evidence': 'Mr Justice Thomas Smyth ... rejected the evidence of Eddie Wilson (Ryanair's head of personnel ...) which he said was "baseless and false"' (Granshaw, 2006: 2).

Commercial aviation is a volatile industry. Bankruptcies are to be expected. Nevertheless the industry's failure to engage in active learning is both dysfunctional and disheartening. Pan Am collapsed in 1991. Swissair and Sabena in 2001. Pan Am's hubris contributed to its downfall. Lessons were there to be learned. But Swissair and Sabena carried on as before believing, as Pan Am had done, that they were invulnerable. They were, after all, *flag carriers*, the very embodiment of their respective nations' noblest values. Being national totems they could expect to be protected, couldn't they?[53]

To paraphrase Schwarz, Swissair suffered from 'overweaning ambition', its staff having 'lost their sense of reality' (how, for example, did Swissair managers come to believe they could turn failing airlines around in the turbulent 1990s?). As with Pan Am remediation came too late. As with Pan Am Swissair lacked the financial, operational, psychological and cultural resources to survive a major crisis (September 11th). As to *why* remediation came too late it may be that Swissair's organisational culture — that of the self-inflated corporation — initially prevented, then retarded active learning. In Sabena's case management's efforts to save the carrier were hampered by industrial strife.

Since September 11th several airlines have failed, including Midway, Ansett, British World and Gill. Others, like BA, Aer Lingus[54] and BMI British Midland,[55] have restructured. Yet others, like Swiss International Air Lines and KLM, have been remodelled by their new partners (Lufthansa and Air France). Each case provides a unique learning opportunity. Passive learning 'where lessons are identified but not put into practice' is insufficient. Only active learning 'where ... lessons are embedded into an organisation's culture and practices' (Department of Health, 2000: ix) can provide a bulwark against malice and misfortune. All airlines, whether long-haul, regional or low-cost, should note the part played by corporate (and possibly national) hubris in the downfall of Pan Am, Swissair and Sabena. Further spectacular and damaging collapses will be avoided only if the industry learns and applies the lessons of the past *in perpetuity*.

Finally, the fact that business-only carriers like Maxjet are today (2006) enjoying a certain success suggests that the concept of quality service is far from dead. Indeed, it would seem to be rather popular with certain types of passenger (business people and those wanting a more exclusive and luxurious experience for themselves and their family). Swissair's problem was that, due to its lack of reflexivity (self-awareness), it failed to deliver its product in a cost-effective manner. The lesson is: when responding to the market (or creating a market) you must do so in a cost-effective way. Employees' two most frequently asked questions should be: 'Am I safe?' and 'Am I efficient?'

8.1 Summary
This study's key lesson is that hubris increases the likelihood of failure (although failure may be delayed through the artifice of subsidy). 'Pride goes before a fall', warns the adage. Indeed it does — especially in the brutal world of commercial aviation. If you want your airline to survive: abandon your ego, be humble, invite feedback, listen, admit your mistakes, correct and *learn* from them ... then repeat this virtuous circle. In the airline business delusions of grandeur are as much a threat to survival as unfair competition, industrial action, avaricious airport authorities, wars, terrorism, high oil prices, accidents, plagues, tsunamis and hurricanes.

References

Airline Business (2006) 'A super cycle?', *Airline Business*, August, p.9.

Airliner World (2002a) 'A Transatlantic Common Aviation Area?', *Airliner World*, January, p. 36.

Airliner World (2002b) 'AEA Sees Poor Traffic Results', *Airliner World*, February, p. 4.

Airliner World (2006) 'THY to Join Star Alliance', *Airliner World*, October, p. 5.

Air Transport Action Group (2000) *The Economic Benefits of Air Transport*, Geneva: ATAG.

AirWatch (1997) 'AirWatch Report — Europe Prepares For Deregulation, March 24'. Reproduced at (2002) http://www.aeroworld.net/31s03247.htm/ January 27.

Ambrose, S.E. (1985) *Rise to Globalism: American Foreign Policy Since 1938*, Harmondsworth: Penguin.

Anselmo, J.C. (2006) 'Fuelling Anxiety', *Aviation Week & Space Technology*, July 31, p.57.

Ashworth, W. (1991) *The State in Business*, Basingstoke: Macmillan.

Baker, C. (2006a) 'Ryanair renews its court battles with Air France', *Airline Business*, July, p. 20.

Baker, C. (2006b) 'Stellar orbit', *Airline Business*, September, p. 46.

Ball, I. (1986) 'Airlines Count Olives', *The Times*, January 25, p. 5.

Barker, S. (2001) 'Swiss state and private enterprise combine to save national carrier', *The Daily Telegraph*, October 23.

Barrie, D. (2006) 'Britannia Blossoms', *Aviation Week & Space Technology*, July 10, p.36.

Barrow, B. (2006) 'Ryanair suing for £3m over security chaos at airports', *Daily Mail*, August 26, p. 4.

Barter, S. (2001) 'Survival of fittest for Euro airlines, 3 October'. Reproduced at (2001) http://news.bbc.co.uk/hi/english/world/europe/ December 12.

BBC News (1999) Swissair crash warning to airlines, January 12. Reproduced at (2001) http://news.bbc.co.uk/hi/english/world/americas/ November 1.

BBC News (2001a) SAirGroup shares nosedive, 12 March. Reproduced at (2001) http://news.bbc.co.uk/hi/english/business/ December 12.

BBC News (2001b) Swissair dives on bankruptcy talk, 11 June. Reproduced at (2001) http://news.bbc.co.uk/hi/english/business/ December 12.

BBC News (2001c) Sabena flies into jobs storm, 9 August. Reproduced at (2001) http://news.bbc.co.uk/hi/english/business/ December 12.

BBC News (2001d) Strikes batter troubled Sabena, 10 August. Reproduced at (2001) http://news.bbc.co.uk/hi/english/business/ December 12.

BBC News (2001e) Swissair grounds all flights, 2 October. Reproduced at (2001) http://news.bbc.co.uk/hi/english/business/ December 12.

BBC News (2001f) Swiss press mourns national symbol, 3 October. Reproduced at (2001) http://news.bbc.co.uk/hi/english/world/europe/ December 12.

BBC News (2001g) Airline collapse shatters Swiss image, 18 October. Reproduced at (2001) http://news.bbc.co.uk/hi/english/world/europe/ December 12.

BBC News (2001h) Belgian national airline bankrupt, 7 November. Reproduced at (2001) http://news.bbc.co.uk/hi/english/business/ December 12.

BBC News (2002) Swiss airline predicts recovery, 13 May. Reproduced at (2002) http://news.bbc.co.uk/hi/english/business/ June 29.

BBC News (2003a) Swiss cuts back on planes, 25 March. Reproduced at (2006) http://news.bbc.co.uk/ August 10.

BBC News (2003b) Huge job losses at Swiss airline, 24 June. Reproduced at (2006) http://news.bbc.co.uk/ August 10.

BBC News (2004) Troubled Swiss turns first profit, 16 November. Reproduced at (2006) http://news.bbc.co.uk/ August 10.

BBC News (2006) 'Airlines terror plot' disrupted, 10 August. Reproduced at (2006) http://news.bbc.co.uk/1/hi/uk/4778575.stm/ August 10.

Bender, M. and Altschul, S. (1982) *The Chosen Instrument*, New York: Simon and Schuster.

Bennett, S.A. (2001a) *Human Error — by Design?* Leicester: Perpetuity Press.

Bennett, S.A. (2001b) 'It's time for Government to help out Rolls-Royce', *Derby Evening Telegraph*, October 27, p. 10.

Bennett, S.A. (2006) *A Sociology of Commercial Flight Crew*. Aldershot: Ashgate.

Branson, R. (2001) 'Pilot of the Jet Age: Juan Trippe. *Time* 100: Builders & Titans — Juan Trippe'. Reproduced at (2001) http://www.time.com/time100/profile.trippe2.html/ October 28.

Bremner, C. (1988) 'Israeli agency "warned Pan Am of lax security"', *The Times*, December 24.

Bremner, C. (1990) 'Glamour of flying comes down to earth', *The Times*, December 18, p. 20.

Brookes, A. (1996) *Flights to Disaster*, Shepperton: Ian Allan.

Buncombe, A. (2006) 'Bush "viewed war in Lebanon as a curtain-raiser for attack on Iran"', *The Independent*, 14 August, p.3.

Calder, S. (2002a) 'British Airways is a national institution — and that is part of its problem', *The Independent: The Thursday Review*, 14 February, p. 4.

Calder, S. (2002b) 'Adventures in economy class', *The Independent*, April 29.

Campbell, A. (2002a) 'Forecast 2002 — Airlines'. Reproduced at (2002) http://www.flightinternational.com/ January 18.

Campbell, A. (2002b) 'Swiss set to join **one**world family', *Flight International*, 2-8 April, p. 24.

Campbell, A. and Kingsley-Jones, M. (2002) 'Rebel Skies', *Flight International*, 9-15 April, pp. 29-39.

Castle, S. (2001) 'Sabena files for bankruptcy as Belgian airline's staff walk out', *The Independent*, November 7, p. 17.

Cook, C. and Stevenson, J. (1996) *Britain Since 1945*, London: Longman.

Cronin, J. (2006) 'Setbacks and success for world airlines, 2 January', *BBC News*. Reproduced at (2006) http://news.bbc.co.uk/go/pr/fr/-/1/hi/business/4529084.stm/ August 10.

Davies, R.E.G. (1972) *Airlines of the United States Since 1914*, London: Putnam.

Davies, R.E.G. (1987) *Pan American: An Airline and Its Aircraft*, New York: Orion Books.

Department of Health (2000) *An Organisation with a Memory*, London: HMSO.

Deppa, J. (1993) *The Media and Disasters: Pan Am 103*, London: David Fulton.

Deutsche Lufthansa AG (2005) *European Commission and US anti-trust approval received for Lufthansa's takeover of SWISS*. Reproduced at (2006) http://www.lufthansa.com/group/ August 16.

De Wulf, H. (2001) 'Huge losses for Sabena despite increase in passengers', *Flight International*, April 10.

Dickey, C. and Nordland, R. (2006) 'The Wider War', *Newsweek*, August 7.

Dienel, H.L. and Lyth, P. (1998) *Flying the Flag: European Commercial Air Transport since 1945*, Basingstoke: Macmillan.

Dixon, T. (2006) 'Maxjet. Transatlantic Business Travel', *Airliner World*, October, pp.74-76.

Doganis, R. (1991) *Flying Off Course. The Economics of International Airlines*, London: Routledge.

Dombey, D. (2001) 'Belgian groups join Sabena jobs plan', *Financial Times*, November 8, p. 23.

Done, K. and Dombey, D. (2001) 'Flying closer', *Financial Times*, November 8.

Dowdney, M. (1998) '7 Minutes From Safety', *The Mirror*, September 4, p. 4.

Duke University (1999) 'Digital Scriptorium'. Reproduced at (2001) http://scriptorium.lib.duke.edu/dynaweb/adaccess/ October 28.

Economist, The (2001a) 'The day the world changed', *The Economist*, September 15, pp. 13-14.

Economist, The (2001b) 'Black Days', *The Economist*, October 6, p. 87.

Economist, The (2001c) 'Turning off the tap', *The Economist*, October 27, p. 97.

Endres, G. (2002) 'Jet lag', *Airline Business*, May, pp. 52-54.

Endres, G. (2006) 'Low-cost carriers make further gains', *Airline Business*, July, p. 21.

Fenton, B. (2001) 'Airlines suffer further blow to ailing fortunes', *The Daily Telegraph*, December 24, p. 3.

Field, D. and Baker, C. (2002) 'The only way is up', *Airline Business*, March, pp. 72-73.

Field, D. (2006a) 'Northwest pilots sack leader', *Airline Business*, July, p. 16

Field, D. (2006b) 'Low-cost rivals rush to expand market share', *Airline Business*, August, p. 13.

Flanagan, T.J. (2000) 'Pan Am World Services'. Reproduced at (2001) http://www.panam.org/ October 28.

Fleck, F., Parsley, D. and Smith, D. (2001) 'Is Swissair the First of Many to go Bust?' *The Sunday Times*, October 7, pp. 6-7.

Flight International (2001a) 'Sabena reveals survival package', *Flight International*, 14 August.

Flight International (2001b) 'Who Pays?' *Flight International*, 18-24 September, p. 5.

Flight International (2002a) 'Family silver'. Reproduced at (2002) http://www.flightinternational.com/ January 18.

Flight International (2002b) 'Point of no return', *Flight International*, 19-25 February, p. 3.

Flight International (2002c) 'No-frill flag flying', *Flight International*, 9-15 April, p. 3.

Flight International (2002d) 'BMI adopts low-cost model', *Flight International*, 18-24 June, p. 7.

Flottau, J. (2006) 'Holding Patterns', *Aviation Week & Space Technology*, September 4, pp. 42-44.

Foulkes, I. (2006) 'Airline that crashed and burned, March 2'. Reproduced at (2006) http://news.bbc.co.uk/go/pr/fr/-/1/hi/entertainment/4763598.stm/ August 10.

FT.com (2002) 'Timeline: Sabena's journey to bankruptcy'. Reproduced at (2002) http://www.FT.com/ January 27.

Gandt, R. (1999) *Skygods: The Fall of Pan Am*, McLean: Paladwr Press.

Gill, T. (1998) 'A leadership role', *Airline Business*, July, pp. 32-35.

Gill, T. (2002) 'New airline Swiss emerges from ashes of flag carrier', *Flight International*, 5-11 February, p. 10.

Granshaw, M. (2006) 'Is this the way to run an airline? *The Log*, August/September, Vol. 67, No. 4.

Guardian, The (2001) 'Irish airline is latest to feel the pinch', *The Editor*, October 13, p. 10.

Hall, W. and Bickerton, I. (2001) 'Bouw set to head new Swiss airline', *Financial Times*, November 8.

Hall, W. and Odell, M. (2002) 'Switzerland pushes to see its flag flying again'. Reproduced at (2002) http://news.ft.com/ft/gx.cgi/ January 18.

Heywood, A. (1998) *Political Ideologies*, London: Macmillan.

Hopkins, N. and Kettle, M. (1998) '229 die as jet crashes', *The Guardian*, September 4, p. 1.

Hudson, K. and Pettifer, J. (1979) *Diamonds in the Sky: A Social History of Air Travel*, London: The Bodley Head and British Broadcasting Corporation.

Husband, S. (2002) 'Giddy heights', *The Independent on Sunday Magazine*, 24 March, pp. 12-15.

Hussey, R. and Ong, A. (1999) 'Putting a price on reputation', *Risk and Continuity*, December, pp. 43-47.

Io Communications (2001) 'Pan Am Documentary Project'. Reproduced at (2001) http://www.iocommunications.com/Pan Am/Proposal/Proposal.html/ October 28.

Ionides, N. (2002) 'Jeanniot slams "ill-prepared airlines"', *Flight International*, 11-17 June, p. 21.

Johnson, R. (2004) 'Cover story: Lord of the wings'. Reproduced at (2004) http://www.timesonline.co.uk/

Johnson, S. (2006) 'Tipping Point', *Newsweek*, August 7.

King, A. (2006) 'Britons will still fly after terror alert — but are wary of Muslims', *The Daily Telegraph*, August 25, p. 4.

Knibb, D. (2002) 'Tempers flare over Fox-Lew Ansett bid', *Airline Business*, January, p. 21.

Lovegrove, K. (2000) *Airline Identity, Design and Culture*, London: Laurence King.

Lucas, J. (1981) *Boeing 747. The first 10 years in service*, London: Jane's.

Maidment, R. and McGrew, A. (1991) *The American Political Process*, London: Sage.

McRae, H. (2001) 'Don't feel sorry for the airlines — they're an industry like any other', *The Independent: The Wednesday Review*, 7 November, p. 4.

Middleton, D. (1986) *Civil Aviation: a design history*, London: Ian Allan.

Milner, M. (2006) 'BA profits up 57% despite "brutal" competition', *The Guardian*, 5 August, p. 25.

Mitroff, I.I., Pauchant, T.C., Finney, M. and Pearson, C. (1989) 'Do (some) organisations cause their own crises? The cultural profiles of crisis-prone vs. crisis-prepared organisations', *Industrial Crisis Quarterly*, Vol. 3, No. 4, pp. 269-283.

Mitroff, I.I. and Pauchant, T.C. (1990) *We're So Big and Powerful Nothing Bad Can Happen to Us*, New York: Birch Lane Press.

Morris, B. (1988) 'How the queen of the carriers fought on to stay aloft', *The Times*, December 23, p. 4.

National Aviation Hall of Fame (1997) 'Trippe, Juan Terry — 1970'. Reproduced at (2001) http://www.nationalaviation.org/enshrinee/trippe.html/ November 1.

Neue Zürcher Zeitung (NZZ) Online (2001) Uncertainty About Swissair Continues, October. Reproduced at (2002) http://www.nzz.ch/english/swiss_week/2001/october.html/ January 22.

Odell, M. (2002) 'September 11 "no excuse" for airline job cuts', *The Financial Times*, June 28.

Orwell, G. (1949) *Nineteen Eighty-Four*, London: Secker and Warburg.

Osborne, A. (2001) 'Ryanair shows way as BA hits turbulence', *The Daily Telegraph*, November 6, p. 34.

Osborne, A. (2002) 'No rights issue says embattled BA', *The Daily Telegraph*, February 5, p. 31.

Osborne, A. (2006) 'In market terms there are worst things than terrorism', *The Daily Telegraph*, August 11, p. B2.

Outlook (2001) 'BA's house broker forecasts life-threatening loss', *The Independent: Outlook*, November 6, p. 17.

Pan American World Airways History (2000) 'Pan Am Firsts'. Reproduced at (2001) http://www.panam.org/pafirsts.asp/ October 28.

Pauchant, T.C. and Mitroff, I.I. (1988) 'Crisis Prone Versus Crisis Avoiding Organisations. Is your company's culture its own worst enemy in creating crises?' *Industrial Crisis Quarterly*, Vol. 2, No. 1, pp. 53-63.

Pauchant, T.C. and Mitroff, I.I. (1992) *Transforming the Crisis-Prone Organisation*, San Francisco: Jossey-Bass.

Penney, C. (2002) 'Swiss Simplicity', *Airliner World*, June, pp. 56-58.

Perrow, C. (1984) *Normal Accidents*, New York: Basic Books.

Petzinger, T. (1995) *Hard Landing: How the Epic Contest for Power and Profits Plunged the Airlines into Chaos*, London: Aurum.

Phillips, D. (2005) 'National pride, missed connections', *International Herald Tribune*, June 11.

Pilling, M. (2002) 'New brand dream', *Airline Business*, April, pp. 40-41.

Pinkham, R. (2002) 'New Focus', *Airline Business*, May, p. 43.

Quinn, J. and Litterick, D. (2006) 'Market shakes off terrorism scare', *The Daily Telegraph*, August 11, p. B1.

Rayko, R. (2002) 'US airlines start to recover', *Flight International*, 15-21 January, p. 26.

Regester, M. and Larkin, J. (1997) *Risk Issues and Crisis Management*, London: Kogan Page.

Rendall, I. (1988) *Reaching for the Skies*, London: BBC Books.

Richards, A. (2002) 'BA suffers biggest loss since Gulf War', *Daily Express*, February 5.

Robinson, J.E. (1994) *American Icarus*, Baltimore: Noble House.

Sage, A., Cleroux, R. and Leathley, A. (1998) 'Crashed airliner had warning over possible faulty wiring', *The Times*, September 5, pp. 1-2.

Sampson, A. (1984) *Empires of the Sky*, London: Hodder and Stoughton.

Schwarz, G. (2002) 'Swissair: The End of a (Too) Proud History'. Reproduced at (2002) http://www.nzz.ch/english/editorials/2002/04/04_swiss.html/ April 4.

Sentance, A. (2001) 'Living with slower growth', *Airline Business*, July, pp. 76-78.

Shanks, N. and Wolff, S. (2006) 'The Liquid Bomb Threat', *Air Safety Week*, August 21, Vol. 20, No. 33, pp. 1-2, 4-5.

Sipika, C. and Smith, D. (1992) *Crisis Management Working Papers Number 1: The failed turnaround of Pan American Airlines*, Liverpool: John Moores University.

Smith, D. (1992) 'The Kegworth Air Crash: A Crisis in Three Phases?' *Disaster Management*, Vol. 4, No. 2, pp. 63-72.

Sobie, B. (2006a) 'Transatlantic all-premium market heats up', *Airline Business*, September, p. 22.

Sobie, B. (2006b) 'Aer Lingus eyes post-IPO expansion', *Airline Business*, October, p. 24.

Sochor, E. (1991) *The Politics of International Aviation*, London: Macmillan.

Sparaco, P. (2006a) 'World Players', *Aviation Week & Space Technology*, July 31, p.53.

Sparaco, P. (2006b) 'In Review', *Aviation Week & Space Technology*, September 4, p. 53.

Sunday Times, The (2001) '1944 and all that', *The Sunday Times*, October 7, p. 7.

Swiss (2002a) 'SWISS — Switzerland's new international quality airline, January 31'. Reproduced at (2002) http://www.swiss.com/index/ April 4.

Swiss (2002b) 'SWISS is ready for take-off, March 26'. Reproduced at (2002) http://www.swiss.com/index/ April 4.

Swissair (1999) 'SR 111 update: Swissair and Boeing to jointly pay any damages'. Reproduced at (2002) http://www.swissair.com/about/media/sr111/press_releases/ January 17.

Swissair (2001) 'Customer confidence in Swissair brand continues to increase — load factor exceeds last year's figures for the first time, December 18th'. Reproduced at (2002) http://srapps.swissair.com/srpress/ January 11.

Swissair (2002a) 'Company Information: Facts & Figures'. Reproduced at (2002) http://www.swissair.com/about/company/index.htm/ January 11.

Swissair (2002b) 'Company Information: History'. Reproduced at (2002) http://www.swissair.com/about/company/index.htm/ January 11.

Swissair (2002c) 'Zurich voters endorse new Swiss airline, January 13'. Reproduced at (2002) http://www.sairgroup.com/apps/media/press/e/ January 17.

Swissair (2002d) 'Good bye'. Reproduced at (2002) http://www.swissair.com/ May 3.

Swissinfo (2001) 'Swissair debacle affects Swiss image abroad, October 13'. Reproduced at (2002) http://www.swissinfo.org/sen/ January 22.

Swiss International Air Lines (2006) 'About SWISS'. Reproduced at (2006) http://yourcountry.swiss.com/ August 10.

Taylor, M.J.H. (1997) *The World's Commercial Airlines*, London: Regency House Publishing.

Toft, B. and Reynolds, S. (1997) *Learning from Disasters*, Leicester: Perpetuity Press.

Tran, M. (1998) ' ... the chequered history of a relatively new airliner', *The Guardian*, September 4, p. 3.

Transportation Safety Board of Canada (2001a) 'Accident Summary'. Reproduced at (2002) http://www.tsb.gc.ca/ENG/TSB_Investigations/Swissair/Site_Pages/Acc_summary/summary.htm/ January 11.

Transportation Safety Board of Canada (2001b) 'Aviation Safety Recommendations. Material Flammability Standards. Investigation Into The Swissair Flight 111 Accident. Occurrence Number A98H0003. TSB A 07/2001'. Reproduced at (2002) http://www.tsb.gc.ca/ENG/communiques/AIR/2001/Swissair_23 August.htm/ January 11.

Transportation Safety Board of Canada (2003) *Aviation Investigation Report. In-Flight Fire Leading to Collision with Water. Report Number A98H0003*. Reproduced at (2006) http://www.bst.gc.ca/en/reports/air/1998/ July 3.

Trevelyan, B. (2001) 'Swissair: Proud past, grim future, 2 October'. Reproduced at (2001) http://news.bbc.co.uk/hi/english/business/ December 12.

University of Miami (1996) 'Pan American World Airways, Inc., Records'. Reproduced at (2001) http://www.library.miami.edu/archives/panam/pan.html/ October 28.

Vaughan, D. (1996) *The Challenger Launch Decision: Risky Technology, Culture and Deviance at NASA*. Chicago: University of Chicago Press.

Wall, R. and Flottau, J. (2006) 'Different Worlds', *Aviation Week & Space Technology*, August 7, p. 50.

Watts, R. (2001) 'Insurance premiums to soar 40pc', *The Sunday Telegraph: Money*, October 21, p. 1.

Wilkinson, P. (1991) 'Pan Am: The Fall of a Legend', cited in Deppa, J. (1993) *The Media and Disasters, Pan Am 103*, London: David Fulton.

Zarifeh, R. (2001) 'Swiss punish banks after Swissair debacle, October 4'. Reproduced at (2002) http://www.swissinfo.org/sen/ January 22.

Appendix

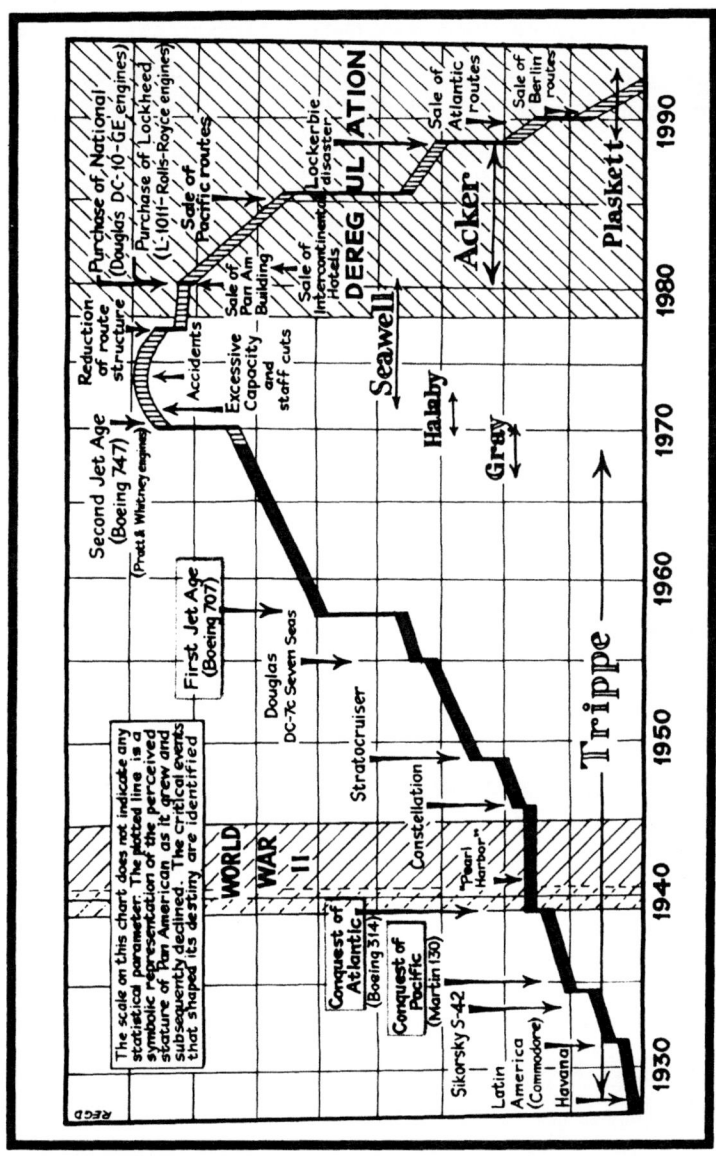

Reproduced with kind permission from *Skygods* by Robert Gandt (1999:2)

The Author
Simon Bennett directs the MSc in Risk, Crisis and Disaster Management at the Civil Safety and Security Unit (CSSU), an element of the Institute of Lifelong Learning. He has been published in *Air Safety Week (US)*, *Focus: Journal of the United Kingdom Flight Safety Committee*, *The Log: Journal of the British Airline Pilots Association*, *Risk Management Bulletin, Science, Technology and Human Values*, *The International Journal of Mass Emergencies and Disasters*, *Risk Management: An International Journal* and other periodicals. His first book *Human Error — by Design?* is available from Palgrave-Macmillan. His second book *A Sociology of Commercial Flight Crew* is available from Ashgate. He is a Member of the Royal Aeronautical Society (MRAeS) and a Fellow of the Institute of Civil Defence and Disaster Studies (FICDDS).

Vaughan College publications
A list of publications is provided on the Institute of Lifelong Learning web site (go to http://www.le.ac.uk/lifelonglearning and select *Books*). Publications may be ordered by printing off the Order Form and returning it to the Institute.

The mission of the Vaughan Papers series is: 'To promote and disseminate the Institute of Lifelong Learning's research, with the aim of encouraging constructive debate on topics of concern to society, and to make academic research, ideas and insights accessible to adult learners and society at large'. Most Vaughan Papers are 5,000 - 10,000 words long. Ideas for new papers should be sent to the Series Editor at sab22@le.ac.uk or Institute of Lifelong Learning, 128 Regent Road, Leicester LE1 7PA. Proposals are considered by the Editorial Board, chaired by the Institute's Professor John Benyon.

Vaughan College was founded as a working men's college in 1862 by David James Vaughan, Vicar of Leicester Cathedral. Renamed Vaughan College in 1908 it became the University of Leicester's Department of Adult Education in 1929. The first Vaughan Paper was A.J. Allaway's *Adult Education in England* published in 1951.

---

[1] Ridley Scott's film *Black Hawk Down* (Columbia-Tristar) explored issues of comradeship and motivation amongst US soldiers and airmen serving in Somalia in the early 1990s.

[2] It remains to be seen whether the changing nature of the terrorist threat (the possible concealment by suicide bombers of explosive devices within the body, for example (Shanks and Wolff, 2006: 2)) will erode the industry's accumulated resilience.

[3] Avoiding a repetition requires that lessons are learned and applied. This is known as 'active learning' (Toft and Reynolds, 1997; Department of Health, 2000).

[4] Given their relatively poor performance, decisions to buy British-made aircraft could only have been made on politico-economic grounds. With a few noteworthy exceptions (like the Viking and Viscount) British designs were late in delivery, failure-prone and relatively uneconomic. Some, like the Brabazon and Saunders Roe Princess flying boat were politically-inspired white elephants (both types were scrapped). Others, like the Hawker-Siddeley Trident and BAC 1-11 were inferior to their American equivalents, the Boeing 727, Boeing 737 and Douglas DC-9 (each of which enjoyed significant sales worldwide). Despite this the government instructed BEA to order Tridents and 1-11s (Ashworth, 1991: 87).

[5] Aviation is far from being a purely commercial pursuit. As *The Sunday Times* (2001) has put it, the 1944 Chicago Convention '... put powers in the hands of government rather than the airlines .... [T]he power of negotiating landing rights and airport slots [belongs to] governments .... Airlines are subject to political bartering, which limits competition'. The aviation industry is *heavily* politicised (Phillips, 2005). Carriers and manufacturers live in the shadow of politicians' ambitions (as evidenced by the rowdy 2006 debate in the French parliament when Airbus's A380 project ran into difficulties).

[6] The rhetoric of the 'democratic mission' is an enduring feature of US political discourse. It was used by President George W. Bush in the aftermath of the September 11th attacks to justify his military expeditions to Afghanistan and Iraq and diplomatic manoeuvrings against the 'axis of evil' (Buncombe, 2006).

[7] See Appendix (Gandt, 1999: 2).

[8] According to Sampson (1984: 127) 'Pan American soon faced a real prospect of bankruptcy'.

[9] The 707 represented a paradigm shift in capabilities. It was nearly twice as fast and could carry about twice as many passengers as the piston-engined aircraft it replaced (such as the Douglas DC-7C, in this author's opinion the apogee of piston-engine-powered passenger aircraft design). It also flew 'above the weather'.

[10] A contemporary UK equivalent would be easyJet.

[11] Trippe had championed the tourist class ticket. The new Pan Am, however, abandoned the mass market. Trippe's patrician populism was ditched.

[12] The price war occurred in an industry plagued by marginal profitability (Doganis, 1991: xiii).

[13] This was not a good business decision. The purchase price was high. National's routes and aircraft were not fully compatible with Pan Am's, and the airline had labour problems. Pan Am inherited 16 DC-10 widebodies powered by engines unfamiliar to Pan Am engineers. The DC-10 complicated Pan Am's operations: the airline had recently ordered 12 Lockheed L-1011 widebodies (Davies, 1987: 82). The L-1011 was the 'alternative' DC-10. It never proved as popular as its rival.

[14] Running an airline with non-airline people is not unheard of. In 2006, for example, two major UK carriers, Virgin Atlantic and easyJet, had generalists in charge (one from the entertainment industry, the other from road transport).

[15] Sabena's pilots reacted in the same way to their CEO's rationalisation plan.

[16] Employee magnanimity is an enduring feature of the US airline industry. In 2006 five thousand members of Northwest Airlines's Air Line Pilots Association accepted a '"deeply concessionary" five-and-a-half year contract entailing pay cuts of 24% and work rule changes' (Field, 2006a: 16).

[17] These divestments raised $900 million. Pan Am also sold its stake in Falcon Jet Corporation.

[18] In purchasing new and efficient aircraft Acker was following industry fashion (Doganis, 1991: 3).

[19] Operating a mixed fleet is generally more expensive.

[20] According to Petzinger (1995: 303) Airbus had used government subsidy to keep prices down.

[21] Some years earlier a Pan Am manager, with Acker's backing, had secured a 10 per cent wage cut 'to save Pan Am'. Employees were promised a restoration of pay levels in 1985 (the 'snapback'). When the snapback date arrived, Pan Am went back on its word. (According to Petzinger management never intended to honour the promise). A bankers' report warned: 'Employees will not trust management until its word can be relied upon' (Petzinger, 1995: 190-191 and 228-229).

[22] In 1986 Pan Am bought Ransome to start Pan Am Express and launched the Pan Am Shuttle.

[23] In 1986, for example, Palestinian terrorists hi-jacked a Pan Am aircraft to Karachi. Seventeen passengers were killed. The next day Arab gunmen killed 21 at an Istanbul synagogue. Reliance on the North Atlantic made Pan Am vulnerable to events in Europe and the Middle East (Sipika and Smith, 1992: 14-17).

[24] This was an interesting decision. One might have expected the Board to support the 'company man' Shugrue over the itinerant Acker.

[25] Pan Am still outlasted its great rival Eastern Airlines which went Tango Uniform in early 1991. Eastern's failure shocked Pan Am's pilots: 'Many believed it would never happen. *Nah, not Eastern, for Christ's sake. Eastern is one of the oldest companies in the business ...* ' (Gandt, 1999: 260).

[26] According to Fenton (2001) 'An estimated 100,000 Americans ... lost their jobs in airlines, hotels and other travel industries'.

[27] By early 2002 plans were being laid to resurrect both Canada 3000 and Ansett — but as 'pared down' operations. In Ansett's case only about 25 per cent of the airline's 16,000 staff would be re-hired (Knibb, 2002).

[28] Sabena, founded in 1923, was Belgium's flag carrier and Europe's second oldest airline.

[29] Both Gill and British World were established independent operators.

[30] As Taylor (1997: 6) explains: 'A major trend for airlines has been to enter into co-operation agreements to co-ordinate aspects of their businesses and reduce running costs, the intention being to share some none-core resources and thereby save money by avoiding too much duplication or spare capacity'.

[31] Despite operating 401 aircraft to 294 destinations The *Quali*flyer Group was smaller than Star Alliance and **one**world.

[32] SAirGroup was formed in 1997 as a 'holding structure' for four corporate divisions: SAirLines; SAirServices; SAirLogistics; and SAirRelations. SAirLines catered 'for all pure-airline activities, including Swissair and Crossair'. Swissair represented about 45 per cent of revenues and 45 per cent of earnings of SAirGroup (Swissair, 2002b; Gill, 1998: 35).

[33] Crossair, SAirGroup's regional subsidiary, suffered the loss of an aircraft after Swissair failed. On November 24 2001 a Crossair Avro RJ100 crashed killing 24 passengers and crew. According to Hall and Odell (2002) this accident further damaged SAirGroup's reputation.

[34] These were major and very public perturbations within the airline's management.

[35] 2000 was a good year generally for the industry. Passenger numbers increased 9 per cent on 1999, although the growth of international passenger traffic slowed.

[36] Sabena was in financial difficulty at this time. It lost £86.9 million in the first half of the year. In August 2001 the airline announced it was cutting 1,600 jobs, reducing its fleet by seven aircraft and disposing of its maintenance, catering and cargo handling businesses. Sabena's CEO, Christophe Müeller stated: 'Without this plan there is no survival .... [Sabena must] get modest again'. At this time about half of Sabena's caterers and baggage handlers were on strike. Around 150 flights had to be cancelled (Müeller, cited in *BBC News*, 2001c).

[37] See Ashworth (1991) for a definition of the 'public corporation'.

[38] Swissair's poor cost control should be kept in perspective. In the financial year 2001-2002 the world's airlines suffered an estimated $12 billion loss, much of it, according to Pierre Jeanniot, attributable to '... the creeping expansion of overheads' (Jeanniot, cited in Ionides, 2002: 21).

[39] Keynesianism means the regulation of economic activity through government intervention. The result is a 'managed economy'. Reaganomics (and Thatcherism, its anaemic copy) is informed by principles of 'laissez-faire' economics, which decry state intervention.

[40] National governments subsidise manufacturers as well. The Canadian government was found guilty by the World Trade Organisation of giving unfair subsidies to its regional aircraft manufacturer Bombardier, and Brazilian manufacturer Embraer accused the German government and state-owned banks of subsidising Munich-based Fairchild-Dornier (which no longer exists) (Endres, 2002: 53).

[41] One of the reasons for Ryanair's success is its investment in fuel-efficient airliners (Wall and Flottau, 2006: 50).

[42] Sabena's divestment programme mirrored that undertaken by Pan Am (to little avail) in the 1980s.

[43] Today (2006) airline alliances are in vogue. Even Japan Air Lines (JAL), for so long an independent operator, has joined **one**world (although Virgin Atlantic and Emirates have chosen to stay independent) (Baker, 2006b: 46).

[44] Like Pan Am, North Atlantic enthusiasts BA and Virgin Atlantic have fallen into the same honey trap. Both airlines have been hit hard by the post-September 11th slump in North Atlantic travel (Field and Baker, 2002).

[45] In its efforts to rebuild, Swiss International Air Lines rationalised its scheduled fleet around just two types, Embraer and Airbus (Penney, 2002: 58).

[46] This is the 'kernel' of the onion model.

[47] Ten people died in the accident on January 10, 2000. Thirty-three died on November 24, 2001.

[48] In November 2001 '... the North Atlantic market continued to be the worst affected with a drop of 31.5%' (*Airliner World*, 2002b).

[49] Four years later the business class-only model came of age with carriers like Maxjet and Eos: 'Competition in the emerging all-premium transatlantic market is heating up with expansion at two fledgling carriers .... Eos and Maxjet ... claim to be enjoying 70 per cent load factors ... ' (Sobie, 2006a: 22). In October 2006 Maxjet claimed load factors in the mid-seventies. It also announced plans to expand its fleet to five Boeing 767s (Dixon, 2006: 74-76).

[50] The success of business-only carriers like Maxjet (which in 2006 claimed load factors of over 70%) would seem to confirm Rattray's assertion.

[51] Ryanair's unique selling point (USP) is that it offers the lowest possible fares. As Comacho puts it: 'Ryanair is an absolute value carrier. Ryanair's prices are not just lower than other carriers' fares — they are simply cheap' (Comacho, cited in Campbell and Kingsley-Jones, 2002: 38).

[52] Following the August 2006 alleged terrorist plot to attack trans-Atlantic flights originating in the UK and consequent additional security measures, Ryanair CEO Michael O'Leary said he would take the British Government to court 'for losses from cancellations and lost bookings ... ' (Barrow, 2006: 4). Interestingly, a poll revealed that '63 percent ... refuse[d] to condemn the way Britain's airports dealt with the situation ... ' (King, 2006: 4). The following outburst illustrates O'Leary's management style: 'Are we going to apologise when something goes wrong? No, we're f***ing not. Please understand. It does not matter how many times you write to us complaining that we wouldn't put you up in a hotel because there was fog in Stansted. You didn't pay us for it' (O'Leary, cited in Johnson, 2004).

[53] The fact that, ultimately, they were abandoned by their respective governments might tell us something about the nature of politics and ability of nations to defy global trends.

[54] Aer Lingus's plight was typical. With high fixed costs, low returns on capital and wafer-thin margins (*The Guardian*, 2001) even minor perturbations threaten survival. In November 2001 Eire's flag carrier was losing IR£2 million daily. The cost of making some 2,000 staff redundant was put at IR£40 million. The airline began selling its art collection to raise money. Like BA and Virgin, Aer Lingus depended on the Atlantic market. By the autumn of 2006, after years of brutal cost-cutting (that reduced unit costs by nearly 50 per cent), Aer Lingus was one of the most efficient airlines in Europe (Sobie, 2006b: 24).

[55] BMI laid off staff and launched a 'low cost' subsidiary, Bmibaby. Cassani warned: '[This tactic] was tried in the US and failed every time' (Cassani cited in Campbell and Kingsley-Jones, 2002: 36). Bmibaby was still operating in 2006, though on a much smaller scale than easyJet and Ryanair.